The Art of Effective Letter Writing

Published by :
Lotus Press Publishers & Distributors

The Art of Effective Letter Writing

Robert Hills

4735/22, Prakash Deep Building
Ansari Road, Darya Ganj,
New Delhi - 110002

Lotus Press : Publishers & Distributors
Unit No. 220, 2nd Floor, 4735/22, Prakash Deep Building,
Ansari Road, Darya Ganj, New Delhi- 110002
Ph.: 41325510, 98118-38000
• E-mail : lotuspress1984@gmail.com
www.lotuspress.co.in

The Art of Effective Letter Writing

ISBN: 81-89093-93-2

Printed & Published by : **Lotus Press Publisher & Distributors,** New Delhi-02

CONTENTS

PREFACE

Letter writing is essential to many tasks, related to business, commerce, government and other important organisations. Every educated person should have the art of writing letters for all occasions for practical reasons.

Communication between men, organisations and so on is quite indispensable, and letters bridge the gap between them. The purpose of writing is to communicate a thought, a fact, an idea, a sentiment, a celebration or a happening. A well constructed letter can help you to win new business, and improve and develop your relationship with clients. A skilful written letter can smooth troubled waters and heal wounded feelings.

This book is designed to provide you with the tools for making letter writing less of a chore, whatever the situation. You will find suggestions and plenty of examples on how to deal with most of the kinds of letter you will have to write.

— **Maya Badri**

1

INTRODUCTION

In this fast-paced world of communication letter writing has become a very important routine function of the private organisations as well as the government departments all over the world.

Most writing is a private activity but a public service. You may dash off a protest letter in the solitude of your study, or apply for a job in response to an advertisement in the newspapers. But in each case, your intention is the same—that eventually your writing will become the reading matter of someone else. Writing letters, in other words, is above all a mode of communication.

The hallmarks of good letter writing are the hallmarks of all good communication. Since letter writing is primarily for communication, you have to keep your reader constantly in mind as you write. This is not always so easy to do. Faced with an intense or convoluted writing task, you may often become very inward looking, struggling to put your thoughts into words and get the words down in your letter. This means taking the trouble to write in the most lucid language.

When writing a letter, keep thinking of the reader's likely response to the contents, the style and the tone. As for the contents, don't, for example, burst into detailed technical explanations, unless the readers are experts. For brevity's sake though, avoid long-winded non-technical explanations.

As for style, take care not to use language that goes over the heads of the readers. For highly educated and well-read prospective readers, don't patronise them by writing in a grossly simplified, plodding style.

As for tone, pitching it correctly is rather like dressing correctly. Use an informal tone for colleagues and familiar people, but use an appropriately respectful and formal tone for bureaucrats, managing directors, officials, etc.

Pay attention also to your layout, to your handwriting or typing, and to your paragraphing. Bear in mind the impression your letter will make.

Careful drafting must be matched by careful presentation. Any letter must be neatly and attractively presented. What you are aiming for in any letter you have to write can be summed up in three words—accuracy, brevity and clarity.

Make sure that you have all the relevant facts. In official letters, make sure that you quote references, names, dates, etc. A strong, clear start to your letter will help both you and your reader to direct your minds to the matter in hand.

Make your letters lean and fit, with plenty of meat and no fat. In short, be brief and concise. Be prompt in replying to letters. Promptness is even more crucial in the personal ones in which you show real consideration for someone—thank you notes, letters of congratulations and best wishes, get-well-soon letters and cards, letters of condolence, and so on.

All good writing follows the same basic principles. Certainly, a business letter is different from a personal one. The difference is what you write about rather than how you write.

The section on personal/social letters includes notes of thanks, congratulations and good luck, get-well-soon letters of condolence, letters of apology and anger, letters of introduction, love letters, invitations and announcements, etc.

The section on business letters covers enquiries and requests, offers and quotations, orders, complaints, claims, credit letters, remittance letters, collection letters, sales promotion letters, circular letters, letters of recommendation and credit, bank correspondence, agents and agencies, life insurance, fire and marine insurance, import and export correspondence, application of employment, letters of introduction and reference, etc.

The last section focuses on official letters to bureaucrats, government officials, members of parliament, etc.

2

THE STRUCTURE OF A LETTER

Letters remain hugely important in our everyday lives. People still feel the need to have something confirmed in writing, and a letter can add the all important touch.

Adopt a letter layout that is clear and consistent. All letters basically have six parts to them. They are as follows:

1. The Heading, consisting of:

   a) the writer's address

   b) the date

2. The courteous Greeting or Salutation
3. The Communication or Message, that is the body of the Letter
4. The Subscription, or courteous Leave-taking, or Conclusion
5. The Signature
6. The Superscription, on the Envelop

Certain types of letters, especially official letters, can have other elements, such as references and the address of the recipient.

THE HEADING

This consists of two parts: the address and the date. It informs the reader where you wrote the letter, and when. The *where* shows your full postal address to which the reader may reply, and the *when* is for reference, as it gives him the date on which you wrote.

The position of the heading is the top right hand corner of the first.

1. The Address

The address is on the top right-hand corner, and the date just below it. If you have headed notepaper, your address is, of course, already there.

A common custom with official letters is to include your name as the first line of the address but it is not necessary in social or friendly letters. In all personal letters, it is usual not to put in your name until you sign it at the end. But it is an optional matter. By all means do so if the letter is more than one page, and is going to someone who will not recognise your handwriting.

> Maya Badri,
>   "Shivam" 17th Main,
>   Banashankari,
>   Bangalore-70

There are three ways to set out the address. Many people prefer the indented form, as shown in the above examples.

There are others who prefer the black form for official letters. In this format, each line begins directly below the one above.

> Mrs. Maya Badri
> "Shivam" 17th Main
> Banashankari,
> Bangalore- 70

The third way is to centre your name and address at the top of the sheet.

Mrs. Maya Badri

"Shivam"

17th Main

Banashankari

Bangalore-70

The commas or full stops at the end of the lines are no longer considered important. If you omit them then the address has a more streamlined look.

When you are on a holiday, away from home, it is not necessary to give an address in letters or postcards, but you ought to give some indication of where you are writing from:

Wellington, 15th April

If you are staying long at a place, and you want your correspondent to reply to you, use the formula 'c/o, (care of)' with the name of the person you are staying with:

C/o Dr Kaushik Kumar

F-17, South Lockey Road

Beacon

New York-12207

2. The Date

In personal letters, it is customary to write the date below the address in the letter. Some prefer to write it at the end of the letter on the left-hand side, alone. You may write just the day and month, and ignore the year, but this is just a matter of choice.

All business letters should show day, month and year. Avoid using the format of 4/2/95 or 4—2—95. Instead write, 4 February 1995 or February 4, 1995. The former is likely to cause confusion, for while in America 4-2-95 stands for April 2, 1995, in the rest of the countries it reads as 4 February 1995.

Write the date below the address. If you use headed notepaper, type or write the date in at the appropriate place.

GREETING OR SALUTATION

The salutation or greeting is at the left—hand of the first page, at least two lines below the last written line before it. It is set flush against the left margin. If you not sure of the name of the person you are writing to, use, "Dear Sir', or 'Dear Madam'

The form of greating will depend upon the relation in which you stand to the person to whom you are writing.

In personal letters, you can vary the salutation as you prefer. To members of your family, you can write:

Dear Mother and Father

My dearest Sandhya

Hello Shubhi!

Dear Uncle

To friends it can be:

Dear Shri Natarajan

Dear Natarajan

Dear Mrs. Rao

A general rule of thumb in cases of doubt is to greet the person with the name you know him or her by. It would be bad form to salute an old friend with 'Mrs. Shiva' if you normally called her 'Pinky'.

To business people, it will be:

Dear Sir

Dear Gentlemen

In the USA, very formal letters carry the salutation:

My Dear Sir

They also use 'Gentlemen' when writing to an organisation. While the practice in most Commonwealth countries is to use a comma after a salutation, in the USA a colon is more common.

The use of the terms 'Dear' is purely formal and a polite expression, not necessarily implying any special affection.

BODY OF THE LETTER

The body is written as text, and is known as the main text. This includes the message you want to write. Normally in a friendly letter, the beginning of each paragraph is indented. Now a days, however, it is common not to indent. In that case, be sure to skip a line between paragraphs. Skip a line after the salutation and before the close.

The body of the letter has three parts:

a) the opening

b) the message

c) the close

The introduction or opening lines of the letter can be:

a) Thank you very much for your kind letter.

b) I am so glad to receive your letter after such a long time!

c) You will be glad to learn that ....

d) What a nice letter from you!

e) I feel so happy to hear of your success!

The message is the main of a letter. Divide your letter into paragraphs to denote changes of subject matter. Keep your paragraphs short, and leave a clear line between two paragraphs.

Use simple language and short sentences. Don't try to impress the other person with a flowery or eloquent language. Be clear about what you want to say, and say it as directly as possible.

Try to write completely what you want to express. Adding postscripts at the end of a letter denotes carelessness and slovenly thinking. Think before you write.

If you are writing the letter, then do so neatly, and in a legible style. Be careful to use punctuation wherever necessary so as to avoid altering the whole meaning of a sentence.

The closing paragraph or sentence should indicate that you have completed what you want to convey to the reader.

SUBSCRIPTION

Leave at least one clear line after the end of the text before putting in the conclusion. The subscription, being a courteous leave-taking, should not end abruptly, with just the writer's name. So certain forms of polite leave-taking are necessary.

The traditional rule is that a letter starting with 'Dear Sir' or 'Dear Madam' ends with 'Yours Faithfully'. You can also use 'Yours truly' though this is becoming obsolete now.

If you start with 'Dear Miss Anisha' or 'Dear Mr. Siddharth', end with "Yours Sincerely".

If you are writing to thank someone for something, you can use 'Gratefully yours' or 'Yours in gratitude'.

The word 'respectfully' is used only by tradesmen to a customer, or by an employee to the boss, Never use closings like 'I have the honour to remain...' and 'Your obedient servant' unless it is an open letter to certain government officials.

Personal letters offer you a wide choice and chance to use your imagination. Your relationship with the reader, and the tone and purpose of the letter will be the key to how you close your letter, such as:

Yours as ever
Best wishes
All the best.
Kind regards.
With thanks
Good luck!
See you soon.
Keep smiling!
Be good.
With love
Remember me to...
Hope to hear from you soon
Please give my love to...
I look forward to hearing from you soon.
Please give my love to...
With regards to.....

Affectionately

In family letters people often sign off with a mention of their relationship to the reader, such as:

Your loving brother/mother/son/father, etc.

Best wishes from your uncle/aunt/cousin

The first word of the subscription must begin with a capital letter.

Sincerely yours

The subscription is normally written at the right-hand side, though these days we see people writing it at the left-hand side, flush with the margin.

Remember that there is no apostrophe in 'Yours'.

THE SIGNATURE

Type or print your name. The handwritten signature goes above this line and below the subscription. The signature line and the handwritten signature are indented to the same column as the close. Leave a three or four—line gap before entering your signature. That way your name will stand out clearly. If you have typed the letter, the signature should be in blue or black ink. If the letter is quite informal, you may omit the signature line as long as you sign the letter.; for example:

a) Yours affectionately

   Maya

b) Yours sincerely

   K. R.Natarajan

If, over the years, your signature has degenerated into a meaningless squiggle, try to rectify it. Make sure it can be read. If you are a woman, you should decide whether you want to include your marital status in your signature. It will be helpful to those who respond to your letter if you include Mrs, Miss, Ms., Smt., Km, in brackets after the surname.

Be sure not to include military, honorific, professional or academic titles and the like in your signature.

THE SUPERSCRIPTION ON THE ENVELOPE

The address on the envelope should be written clearly. If necessary, print in block capitals. This may be spaced and punctuated in either of the following ways:

Shri Badri Natarajan,

2539, Safdarjung Road,

Srirampur,

Hyderabad-18

Or

Shri Badri Natarajan,

2539 Safdarjung Road,

Srirampur,

Hyderabad-18

Some business addresses can be very long when you have to include the job title and department. In such cases, you can combine elements on one line without causing confusion. Let the name remain in its own line, and make sure all other important elements stand out.

Mrs Margaret Thomas,

Executive Manager, Sales Department,

Hindustan Metals Corporation,

Navi Mumbai

When you are writing a personal letter to a friend at work, you ought to put 'personal', 'private and confidential', etc. at the top left corner of the envelope. If you want to write 'please forward, write it at the top or bottom left corner.

The thing most often forgotten on envelopes is the return address. This ensures that if the letter does not reach the person you addressed it to, you will get it back, making you realise that your party has not received it. The return address can be on the top left corner, or the back flap.

PART I
SOCIAL LETTERS

3

PERSONAL / FRIENDLY LETTERS

Social letters includes invitations and replies, letters of congratulations, thank you notes, letters of condolence, friendly letters, etc. While personal letters are informal, the others are formal.

Personal letters are written in the manner of one person speaking to another, for they are very informal letters. Such letters have no strict rules or style, not even grammatical rules. Personal letters may be handwritten or typed, but they are always signed by hand.

As you sit down to write a letter to a friend look in your heart and express yourself. Pause and think deeply about your friend. Write to him or her with sincere feelings.

Generally, it is not difficult knowing what to write. There is often some special reason for writing—to thank someone for a gift, to condole a friend who has lost someone dear. You need to write as if you are talking directly to that person. As ever, it pays to give a little thought to content beforehand, and to arrange it into some kind of order. Then quickly write it down. This is your chance to let your full personality come across.

Though your letter may say a lot about yourself, it should start and end with the person you are writing to. The easiest way to do this is to ensure that the word 'you' or 'your' occurs in the first and last sentences.

Even in the main body of the letter, avoid writing too much about yourself. If it is a long letter, come back to the recipient every now and then. Even if you have lots of news to give, split them into small paragraphs. Try avoiding a string of sentences beginning with 'I'—this smacks of self-centredness.

Write letters in an easy, conversational style. They are really in a friendly chat form, being spontaneous and unpremeditated, just as in friendly talk. You can touch on many subjects and in order of your preference, as you remember things. But this does not mean you can be careless and slovenly in dashing off letters without a little thought to style, expressions, and some order in expressing thoughts.

Another point to be taken care while writing it in a free and easy style is to give thought to the basic rules of spelling, punctuation, grammar and unnecessary use of idioms.

In friendly letters to relatives and close friends, the proper form of address is the first name (without title) of the person to whom you are writing, prefixed by such qualifying terms as 'Dear', 'My dear', My dearest...' etc.

The subscriptions are also different to close friends and relatives you can write, 'Yours affectionately', 'Your loving daughter' , 'Yours very sincerely', (to friends) 'With love and best wishes' 'From your loving friend'.

If you address the person as 'Mr.' or 'Shri', then close with 'Sincerely' or 'Very sincerely', and this may be preceded by 'With kind regards'.

From a girl to her friend, telling her about her meeting with a famous cricketer.

14, Shivaji Road,
Rangpura
Cuttack-15
10 June, 2005

My dear Aruna,

You can't guss who I met yesterday! Rahul Dravid ! I had been to Botanical Garden with two of my friends. We saw Rahul standing under a tree, and surrounded by a few cricket fans.

We too went along to see him. He saw us and smiled at us as we approached him. Encouraged by his smile, I took courage, went up to him and extended my hand out for a handshake. And he obliged !

Oh, I am so thrilled! I wish you too had been here, especially as you too are an ardent fan of his. Better luck next time!

When are you returning to Cuttack? I miss you. Do come soon.

Yours affectionately

Maya

Remember too, when you are answering a letter, to pay attention to what it had to say. This will ensure that the receiver knows you are serious about what you reply. If there is something not clear in the letter, ask about it. Comment on the various pieces of news that it contained. If there were any questions asked, be sure to answer them.

Aruna's reply

310/A, Hilton Apts,
N R Mohalla
Aligarh-16
14 June, 2005

My dear Maya,

Thank you very much for your very interesting letter. I do envy you ! You really must have been thrilled meeting Rahul Dravid! How I wish I too had been there with you to meet him! Hopefully, I will meet him one day.

I am returning to Cuttack on 25 June. By then I would have finished visiting all my relatives. I have yet to see my brother who is arriving from Germany tomorrow. I am meeting him after five years! He will be with us for a week this time before he goes to Indonesia, and then Australia.

Do you want anything from here? Please let me know soon if you do so.

With regards to your parents, and love to you.

Yours affectionately,
Aruna

Always remember that writing gives a touch of permanence to matters that are otherwise likely to be forgotten.

4

THANK YOU LETTERS

Very few people are comfortable with writing thank you letters. And yet you do have to thank the person for his hospitality or other favours rendered to you; this is a basic common courtesy.

What most people consider to be a problem—of writing thank you letters—is only imaginary. You might feel that when you write something like, 'Thank you for the nice lunch, it was lovely!' it may sound brusque, but it is definitely better than saying nothing.

Thank you letters need not be long. You can be brief in your thanks but be sincere about it for this more than makes up for the brevity.

It is easier to write thank you letters or notes for presents or special favours like hospitality. But it is quite easy to forget to thank those who have spared you their precious time over long periods, like teachers, colleagues, parents, siblings, servants, etc. These people too deserve your thanks, and a letter thanking them will touch them even more when unexpected.

A teacher who taught you in the necessary class, and now retired, might be overwhelmed by your gesture when you send her/him a thank you letter.

You too get the feeling of having accomplished something worthwhile.

Mayfair Cottage
21, Links Road,
Mussouri-2
3 April,1998

Dear Mrs. Leslie,

I have been remembering you a lot since I left your class way back in my nursery class. But I have not ever forgotten how kind and gentle you were with me, especially when I cried for my mummy. You taught me to be brave and confident, which has stood me so well in all my formative years. Today, I remember all that you taught me which has stuck with me, and still prove useful.

I trust you are well and enjoying your retirement.

With best wishes

Your loving student
Krishna

Sometimes, the most difficult task in writing a thank you letter is what to say. Several easy variations could be:

a) It is really a delight to...

b) We enjoyed the party/trip/present very much. What a lovely idea!

c) We cannot thank you enough for......

d) It is not stretching the truth to say that, thanks mainly to you, the journey was the best yet....

e) We are most indebted to you for your thoughtful gesture in....

f) You have been a great source of help to us, and we would like to thank you for....

After writing this, very little more need be said, but if you want you can fill in with a few pieces of personal news, if the receiver happens to be a friend or relative.

The thank-you letters that you write to people whom you know socially should be hand-written. It makes them more personal.

"Shreyas"
15, Janakidas Road,
Begumpet,
Hyderabad-10
15th May,1999

Dear Uma,

It was so nice and thoughtful of you to visit me here at the hospital. It cheered me up very much. Life here becomes so dreadfully monotonous, in spite of the efforts of the nurses to cheer me up. So your visit was a wonderful surprise, and the bouquet of roses plus the magazines have brightened and cheered me up a lot. I am feeling a lot better now, and hopefully should be discharged in another two or three days. I am eagerly waiting to go home. If you happen to come this side, do drop in at the house.

Once again, thanks for taking the time to visit me here.

Affectionately,
Priya

When you receive gifts or presents, a thank you letter should be written within a couple of days of receiving them. The letter can be brief, thanking the person for the present (name the present), and writing a word or two about how much the present is appreciated. You can add other news also if you want.

Dear Rekha,

Thank you ever so much for the wonderful set of pens you sent with your card. It has come in handy as I was planning to buy a good pen soon. I like the different colours of the pens, and will treasure them, especially as they are from a wonderful friend like you.

I have a written test next week as a preliminary stage for an interview with Air India. Your pens will be useful. I'm sure they will bring me luck too!

Many thanks, once again.

Your loving friend
Rashmi

Even young children should be persuaded to write thank you notes. Inculcating this habit at a young age will help in moulding their character into better beings.

Dear Uncle and Aunt

Thank you very much for the quiz books that you presented to me. I like them very much, and they will be of use to me.

Lots of love,
Siddharth

After big events and occasions, like weddings, child-naming ceremony, etc., sending out thank you notes can be a long and tedious affair, but must be done. Try not to delay the writing and be meticulous in acknowledging all the gifts.

Generally, wedding presents given to the bride and the groom should be acknowledged by them, probably after their return from their honeymoon, definitely within two months of their marriage. If the bride is writing, she should include her husband's name, and vice versa. Where the present is from good friends of both, they can both sign, and the letter can be sent to the whole family.

Dear Mr. Rao,

It was most thoughtful of you and Mr. Rao to present us the beautiful cutlery set. They will be most useful for us when we set up our new house.

It was sad that you were unable to attend our wedding, but I hope you will visit us some day and have lunch or dinner with us.

Rahul sends his thanks and greeting and so do I.

Yours sincerely,
Mita Chopra

This is a formal letter. The following letter is an informal one to a close friend.

Dear Chetak

Many, many thanks for the lovely bedspreads, and for attending our wedding, I know that you have very good tastes in selection of particular items suited for particular persons. Your gift is most useful, especially as we are about to set up our new house together. These will remind us of you constantly.

We hope you will visit us soon, and see for yourself how we have arranged and decorated our house.

With love from
Ashwin and Shama

When you return home after spending a few days in someone's house you ought to write and thank your hostess. Known as 'bread-and-better ' they can be problematical, for often you do not know the people well. Your note can be brief, but informal.

Dear Mrs Chawla,

Thank you very much for accommodating us in your house for three days. We are very grateful for your hospitality, and we enjoyed staying with you, Mr. Chawla and the children. You went out of your way to cook such delicious dishes, and to show all the places of interest. We found you and Mr. Chawla to be very friendly and warm, and we are very happy to have got to know you. We would be very happy if you could make a trip here to Boston, and stay with us, so that we can reciprocate your kindness and generocity

Please convey our love to the children and our thanks and regards to Mr. Chawla.

Yours sincerely,
Madhu Kapoor

Remember your letter should have the ring of sincerity in it. When you write a letter of thanks after you have stayed with people who are going to figure large in your life, for example, your prospective parents-in-law, take special care how to word it.

Dear Mr. & Mrs. Abraham,

When Mary told me that I should visit you both, I was very apprehensive. Parents are not always thrilled to meet the people their children bring home.

Needless to say, my apprehensions were unnecessary. You both were so happy and warm in your welcome, so cheerful, that I realised you were the ideal people to have as one's in-laws. I enjoyed the weekend with you, and sincerely hope that we get to know each other better in the times to come.

Thank you very much for making me feel so wanted in your home.

Yours sincerely
Jacob Andrade

There may be times when pressure of work, or some other matter may force you to decline an offer of hospitality. Yet it is incumbent on your part to send a letter of thanks for the offer.

Dear Karan,

It was very nice of you to have sent me a letter inviting me to the gathering at your place during the weekend. I really would have loved to come and meet all our folk. But Jagan has an entrance exam for Medicine on Monday, and he needs some coaching from me. But it was very kind of you to think of us. Please pass on our greetings to the assembled party. I am sure you will have a gala time !

With best wishes,
Madhav

5

LETTERS OF CONGRATULATIONS AND GOOD LUCK

It is always a pleasure sharing in the good fortunes of others. What better pleasure than to receive messages of congratulations!

When you hear some good news, do immediately send off a congratulatory note to the person concerned. The note need not be long, but has to show a sincere appreciation of the achievement, whether it is an engagement, a birth of a child, a promotion, passing an exam, purchase of a new house, etc.

Congratulations on births are usually very short, but a bunch of flowers or an article of clothing will more than make up. Such notes are generally handwritten. You may even send a card, but avoid tasteless and garish ones.

Dear Meenakshi and Rohit,

Many congratulations on the birth of your little son. I hope he doesn't give you sleepless nights!

We will come and see you during the weekend.

Sleep and relax all you can now. It will be the last chance you get for the next few years!

With love,

Bina

You can add a touch of humour in the letter, but don't try so hard as to sound pompous or heavy-handed.

When you send letters and cards carrying good wishes, keep them short, but show that your hopes for the reader are sincere. Be encouraging.

> *Dear Dinesh,*
>
> *Just a note to wish you every success in the forthcoming exams. I am sure you will fare really well , having known you since your formative years. You have done very well all these years, and I am sure, you will continue to do so.*
>
> *Good luck and lots of cheer !*
>
> *Affectionately*
> *Raju Mama*

Regardless of whether you write directly to the person being complimented or to whom you are sending good wishes, the tone should be warm, personal, and relatively informal.

The three essential steps to building your own complimentary letters are as follows:

1. State the reason for the compliment.

Examples

a) I appreciated your outstanding performance in the schoolplay. The director made the right move when he cast you as Shylock.

b) We are proud to have such an outstanding design team working on our product. You truly deserved the Pegasus Award for the best performance of the year.

c) I had the pleasure of reading your latest article, and enjoyed it tremendously. You have a great talent for capturing the humour in everyday life.

d) Many of you may not know that we have a hero in our midst, Last Saturday Raghav rescued two children from a sinking boat.

e) We want to tell you how proud we are of you for your

outstanding achievement in obtaining your doctorate in the field of microelectronics.

Some of the following phrases may come in handy:

A job well done

Could not imagine a more deserving

Delight ed to hear...

Had the pleasure of...

Heartiest congratulations!

How much I appreciated...

Just learned of...

May not be aware...

Not surprised...

This significant accomplishment...

This prestigious award...

Very proud of ...

Was happy to learn of your outstanding performance/ achievement...

2. Acknowledge the personal qualities required to reach the achievement or accomplishment.

Examples

a) His actions are a reflection of the courage and unselfishness that we have come to recognise in him.

b) I know how difficult it must have been to work part- time, go to school full-time, and still set aside quality time with your family. You are an excellent example to us all.

c) This is a significant accomplishment that undoubtedly by required the dedication and cooperation of the whole team.

d) It is a tribute to your administrative talent and your hard work.

e) You must have spent weeks travelling the by-lanes of our states to gather the stories you wove together so skilfully.

The following phrases may be useful :

Worthy role model

Desire for success

Developed your talent for

Earned the respect of

Fortitude and perseverance

Genuine caring for

Has a gift for

Has the determination to

Inherent desire to achieve

Knowledge and experience

Outstanding talent

Perseverance and sheer hard work

Person of unquestioned integrity

Presence of mind

Set a fine example for

Stand up for what is right and fair

The courage to keep going

Willingness to dedicate yourself to

3. Extend your wishes for continued success.

Examples

a) We wish you similar success in the future.

b) I commend you for your achievement, and hope you will enjoy its rewards for years to come.

c) We compliment on your success, and send our best wishes for the future.

d) We appreciate your devotion :o your position, and wish we had more leaders like you.

e) I admire your stamina and ambition. Good luck with your next project.

f) Please accept our compliments and wishes for your happiness and success.

The following phrases can be used:

Appreciation for

Are very proud of you

Cannot estimated the value of.

Commend you for

Continue to excel

Enjoy the reward of

Good luck with

Have my full support

Keep up the good work

Wish you continued success

Your devotion to

Your many contributions to

Your future endeavours

6

GET-WELL-SOON LETTERS

When you are ill, one of the worst things to happen is that it cuts you off from normal life. At such a time a letter from anyone, wishing you speedy recovery, can be such a great consolation. Knowing that people are thinking of you and wishing you well makes you feel connected to them and not lonely. The same feeling exists in people who are working away from home, or with lonely jobs in isolated places. A letter to them peps them up.

There was a time when writing letters was our only means of communicating over long distances. In today's world, we can pick up a phone and speak to anyone in a second or two. Most people prefer to use the phone when they have something to say. Speed and ease of use are the main reasons. Whether personal or business-related, people pick up a phone before they pick up a pen (or sit down at their word processor.

The proliferation of long distance service has brought the cost of speaking out-of-state friends down drastically, giving us yet another reason to pick up the phone instead of writing. Interacting is an important component of communication. However, there are times when writing is better.

Sure, it is nice to here say, 'Honey I love you .' But to read it in a letter, knowing someone took the time to write it, makes it much more meaningful, it is permanent. And even if, at some time in the future, they take these words back, you still have a permanent record of it. Once written, you can read it over and over again, and cherish it time after time, knowing that someone cared enough to take time to write. After all, writing is not an automatic response. It requires thought and consideration, effort, and concentration too.

But the phone is not the only reason that people have stopped writing. The greeting card, the get-well-soon card—these have usurped letter writing. Is there something meaningful you need to say?

"Happy Birthday", "Get-Well-Soon", "I miss you" "Sorry", etc. are just some of the cards available today. Granted, they are nice gestures, but they are still somebody else's words. You can send these cards, but do write a note or letter to say it in your own words as well.

Imagine, cards and letters filled with genuine sincerity from both the author and the sender—you. Try it, and you will like it, and so will the person who is lying forlorn in his bed, trying to get better.

The process of writing letters to sick people is rather different from that of writing normal letters. If you know the person well, try to write frequent letters to cheer him up. The advice to keep things brief does not apply here. The more the better. Use large handwriting to make your letter to the invalid easy to read.

Try to keep the matter light and cheerful. Jokes and bits of interesting news from around the world will make your letter of more interesting. Avoid comments on the invalid's illness, unless you are sure it is not bad.

My dear Vivek

Daya told me this morning that you have been admitted into the hospital for a minor surgery. I am sure you are in good hands of the reputed doctors there. It is a good hospital where the post—operation care is said to be excellent.

I wish you all the best, and hope you have a good and speedy recovery.

I will drop by after your operation. Till then, all the best.

Yours affectionately
Mathew

7

LETTERS OF CONDOLENCE

One of the most meaningful acts of kindness you can do for a mourner is to write a letter of condolence. The words of sympathy and memory are comforting to the bereaved. More importantly, mourners are very appreciative that you took the time to sit and compose a personal message to them, or share a memory of the deceased.

A good condolence letter has two goals: to offer tribute to the deceased, and to be a source of comfort to the survivors. The best letters are like conversations, as if you were talking during a visit. Most often they are written to the bereaved person to whom you feel closest, although it could be a letter to the family.

A condolence letter should be written and sent promptly, generally within a week after the death. Use any standard stationery or letter paper, and write it by hand.

The following are some specific guidelines for writing a good condolence letter:

1) Acknowledge the loss and name the deceased. This sets the purpose and tone of the letter. Let the bereaved know how you learned of the death, and how you felt upon hearing the news. Using the name of the deceased is a tribute that comforts most mourners.

2) Express your sympathy. Use words of sympathy that remind the bereaved that they are not alone in their feelings of sadness and loss.

3) Note special qualities of the deceased. Acknowledge those characteristics that you cherished most about the person who has died. These might be the qualities of personality, like courage and sensitivity, or attributes that are funny or affable, or ways the person related to the world, like being religious or devoted to community welfare.

4) Recall a memory about the deceased. Talk about how the deceased touched your life. Try to capture what it was about the person that you admired, appreciated or respected.

5) Remind the bereaved of their personal strengths. Bereavement often brings with it self-doubt and anxiety about one's own personal worth. By reminding the bereaved of the qualities they possess that will help them through this period, you reinforce their ability to cope. Qualities to mention might be patience, optimism, religious belief, resilience and competence. If you recall something the deceased used to say about the mourner in this regard, you will really be giving the bereaved a gift.

Example

> *...I was impressed by the devotion you and your family evidenced during the period of Shyam's illness. Your care and attention were only one indication of your love for him...*

6) Offer help, but be specific. "If there is anything I can do, please call ," actually puts a burden on those in grief who may be totally at a loss about what needs to be done. A definite offer of help is more appreciated. Whatever you offer, do it. Don't make an offer you cannot fulfil.

7) End with a word of sympathy. Somehow, 'sincerely', 'love' or 'fondly' don't quite sound befitting. Try one of these: "You are in my thoughts and prayers," or "My fond respects to you and yours."

8) If you don't have enough to say for a formal condolence letter, you may prefer to send a sympathy note. These are shorter communications that can be written on personal stationary or added to a commercially available card. As with a condolence letter, the major goal is to offer a tribute to the deceased, and offer comfort to the bereaved.

It often happens that you do not know the person you are writing to. You knew the person who died, but not the family. Introduce yourself in the fewest words possible before offering your tribute.

Dear Mrs Nanda,

I was very sorry to read the death of your husband in today's 'The Hindu'. It came as a great and sad shock.

You won't know me. Your husband was my manager at the Mumbai branch when I started working for the company, but I was moved to my current branch seven years ago. Like everyone else I shall always remember your husband for his kindness and understanding. But I have special reasons to feel grateful to him.

The beginning stage in one's career can seem quite daunting and unnerving, but your husband's trust and confidence in me made my days at work easy. He helped me when I was dealing with a particular set of people who opposed my method of working.

Now that I have people working under me, I hope I show the same tolerance and kindness to them.

Please let me know if you want legal help regarding clearance of papers in the company.

Yours sincerely,
Prithvi

If you are sending a letter of condolence when the deceased died after long suffering, then it is somewhat different.

Dear Sailesh,

I know you must be mourning the death of your mother. She had suffered for so long that death must have come as a mercy to her. We remember her with affection, and she was always in our thoughts.

A mother's death leaves a great void in one's life, and the only consolation is now she is eternally out of further misery.

We can take care of your child, Nikhil, while you visit Haridwar. Please do feel free to let us know how else we can help you.

With sincere sympathies to you and Meera.

Yours sincerely,
Hitesh

8

LETTERS OF APOLOGY AND ANGER

Wish you had not said or done something? A carefully worded apology letter can help smooth things over.

Writing an apology letter shortly after the offence can usually help save a relationship before a wound becomes a scar, and the damage becomes irreparable. You can usually find forgiveness and understanding if you freely acknowledge what you did wrong, and express sincere regret in your apology letter.

Depending on the situation, if you offer the injured party the appropriate material restitution for whatever loss they incurred because of you, this will also help to repair your relationship.

You can help to rebuild your credulity in your apology letter if you can assure the injured party that they will see a definite change in your behaviour, that you truly value their friendship and do not want to lose it

You may find that if you freely apologise and accept responsibility for what you did the injured party may also accept some responsibility for the problem and apologise to you in return.

Be careful, use wisdom in deciding when to write your personnal apology letter. What does your experience with the injured party tell you? Should you write the apology letter immediately or should you wait and give him a brief cooling off period?

Some tips for writing a personal apology letter are:

1) Write this apology letter carefully on a piece of stationery, and don't type it on a computer.
2) Express your apology in the beginning of your letter, "I am sorry" or "I want to apologise..."
3) State exactly what you did wrong early in the apology letter, "I shouldn't have lost my temper when..." or "I have looked all over but I am afraid I have lost your book."
4) Accept responsibility for what you did, and don't blame the other person, "I accept full responsibility for what happened..." or "I know this was completely my fault..."
5) Promise in your apology letter not to repeat your offensive action, and ask the injured party to give you an opportunity to prove this to them.
6) Suggest that the two of you get together at a restaurant or some other non-threatening place so that you can apologise in person and begin to rebuild your relationship.

Letters of apology should be short and to the point, and normally written by hand.

Dear Mr Joseph,

The children have just come in, and they tell me that while playing outside, their ball broke one of your window panes. I do apologise for this accident, but I shall get it replaced immediately. I am bringing with me today a person who will check the measurements of the window pane, and by evening he will have it fixed.

I assure you it won't happen again.

Yours sincerely
Arman Khan

There are times when you want to give a piece of your mind to someone—someone who has spread some malicious gossip about you, someone who has cheated you, your child who has failed in same subject, etc.

The best way to handle this would be to confront the person and thrash things out face to face. This is not always possible. You may never again want to see the person again, so you may feel that putting it in a letter form would be preferable.

Before writing a letter with rebukes or accusations, decide exactly what effect you want to produce, and choose your words accordingly. Read it before you seal it. By taking this precaution you might save a great deal of hard feelings.

Be tactful even when your intention is to find fault. Tone down your criticisum as you don't want to make a permanent enemy of the person you are writing to

"I find it difficult to believe that you, of all people, would say such things of me..."

"It would be such a shame if we fell out over such a trivial matter...."

" I fear you are mistaken...."

"You must have misunderstood...."

These types of sentences suggest that the reader is a decent sort of person, and that what he has done to upset you is out of character. By such framing of sentences you will encourage him to write a letter of apology to you at once.

Play safe by avoiding open rudeness and accusations which may only lead to aggravation, if not litigation. It is far more effective to use wit, coolness, reasonableness, etc., than open hostility and rudeness. It is even better to break off relations completely with cold precision than rude and extreme anger: "I have tolerated enough of your comment. Our friendship is now terminated."

Just suppose a friend who had borrowed money from you finds excuses for not repaying it. You can write a letter to him expressing warnings without threats and recriminations, and this should have the desired effect.

Dear Mohan,

I am sorry that I am forced to write this letter, but I you have to realise this is a serious matter. I have repeatedly been asking you to return the loan of Rs. 5,000. You have been promising to repay it within a couple of days, but there is no sign of it. I am still waiting to hear from you.

Since you have been a very good friend of mine, and a man of integrity and honour, I lent you the money when you needed it urgently. You did promise to return it within 10 days. Now it is nearly six months. It would be a shame if a small disagreement were to come between us, and I can only imagine that you don't realise how important this matter is to me. Or maybe there is some valid reason why you have not returned my money, in which case you ought to tell me.

Please reply.

Saurav

❖ ❖ ❖ ❖ ❖

9

LOVE LETTERS

It has been said that love letters contain words that are the most often kept and the most often burnt.

A love letter is an expression of feelings for another person, which contain your most inner feelings. It may be a forum to move your love for that special person to the next level of intimacy.

When you decide the time is right to express your feelings for that special man or woman, there are several creative ideas you may want to incorporate into your letter for added impact.

The letter you write should come from the heart. Do not worry if you are not a professional writer. What is important in the letter is that you are sincere, honest and caring. Some basic rules should be followed in writing the love letter.

Consider writing the letter in your own handwriting on a special paper. It is difficult to describe the impact this type of presentation makes to your loved one. It is not uncommon for the recipient of such a letter to have the letter framed and displaced in a special place in their home.

Another suggestion for the presentation aspect of the letter is the addition of a small photograph glued to the top of the letter. This allows the recipient to view the photograph and reflect on you with fondness as he/she admires your letter content.

Spelling accuracy is an absolute must when writing any letter. Misspelled words are symbols of carelessness which can distract your message. Consider the message you may be sending to your loved one, when you do not take the time to look up a questionable word in the dictionary.

With regards to content, you should write from the heart with layman terms. Avoid large complicated words when a single and simple one would do.

The opening and closing of the love letters are very important as they set the tone for the entire letter.

Determine the stage of your love. For example, you would not want to start a letter with, "My darling love, Arthi" if you have only dated her for two weeks. A more appropriate opening may be, "To Arthi, with warmest affection."

The opposite rule would apply if your love has moved into a more intimate area. You would not want to write a lesser opening and risk sending the wrong signal to your lover that may suggest you are only friends.

When closing the love letter, it should add impact that sums up your feelings in a few words.

Examples

Yours unconditionally.....

Your beloved husband....

My love...

With heartfelt love....

I long for your touch, love...

Closings of lesser impacts may include such phrases as:

With warmest regards....

With affection...

With fondest memories....

Until our next meeting.....

Yours truly................

Above all, have fun with writing to the person of your dreams. Think of the smile it would bring to your loved one to find a special letter from you under her/ his pillow.

These letters are cherished by the recipient, and often kept for a lifetime. Tap into your creativity and use your imagination.

Love letters are a wonderful way to express your feelings to someone. They are not hard to create, if you give it some thought. Be sincere, a little unique, and you will certainly bring a smile to your love's face, and a joyous flutter to the heart.

Do not use canned poetry. Everyone copies some romantic verse from a famous author to put in his/her love letter. Be different and original. Write your own poem, or, if you are not talented at that sort of thing, simply put down a few lines from the heart about how you feel.

Use a blank card. Instead of adding your verse to a card that already has a saying in it, or putting it on a blank piece of paper, try using a blank card.

Include a small present, something that can be put inside the card or letter. A pressed flower, a small, flat pendant like a gold heart, a memento from some place special you two went on a date, perhaps with the word 'remember' printed on it.

Like all personal letters, love letters should be handwritten.

Dearest Shilpa,

I went to the park nearby, and it reminded me so much of the one we visited while we were at Munnar. The same kind of trees under which there are benches, the small pond around which beautiful flowers grow, the ducks in the pond looking so pretty. I wish you were here with me now. How I miss you!

Everything is fine here but it could be better and you know why. I would gladly send you the money for the ticket if you could get away from there!

Anyway, think about it!

With heartfelt love,

Yours ever,

Deepak

10

LETTERS OF INTRODUCTION

A letter of introduction is a special favour that should be given only to good friends, who you feel sure will get on well with the people you are introducing them to. Also remember that you are imposing a responsibility upon the recipient of the letter to meet and entertain the people you are introducing.

It is not wise to ask for a letter of introduction. Let your friends decide whether they want to introduce you to other friends.

When writing a letter of introduction, you may not want to inform the person being introduced about the letter, thus keeping him in the dark. Suppose your cousin is attending a seminar in Hyderabad, and you have old friends who live there. You write them a letter telling them when and where your cousin will be staying, and ask them to contact him.

But don't tell your cousin that you have written. This leaves your friends free to either meet your cousin or ignore your request if, for whatever reason, they want to.
And in your letter to your friends, tell them something about your cousin, and why you think they might get on well with him.

While this is the modern way of doing things, in the old-fashioned method, the procedure here is to write two letters, one to send by mail to the hosts telling them of the visitor's arrival and the other the actual letter of introduction which the visitor carries with him. This is a short note to the hosts, introducing the visitor, which he presents on arrival.

The main flaw in this method is that the hosts are not left with a choice in offering hospitality. The older generation people, though, still prefer this method. The following is an example of a letter you might give to a friend to present to the hosts.

Dear Shubha

I am handing over this note to Prema, an old friend of mine, who is visiting Bareilly for a few days to stay with her aunt. She is a very friendly person and very humorous. She will be able to tell you all kinds of news about events in your old home town.

I am sure you will be pleased to meet her, and hope you will be able to get together.

Best wishes,
Jamuna

Remember that as with all other letters delivered by hand, you should not seal the envelope. This is an old-fashioned courtesy which allows the bearer of the letter to read what has been written about him.

11

REQUESTING LETTERS

It is human nature to find it easier asking favours for another than for yourself. A 'request' or 'begging' letter requires a lot of tact and careful wording.

Whatever request you want to make, get it over near the start of the letter. Don't be shy or coy. It is better to talk about money rather than financial assistance or your help. Quote the exact amount you require, giving particulars of the amount that need to be settled against the particular debts. Be honest about the likelihood and date of payment.

It would also be better to include other bits of news in the letter, so that you don't appear totally mercenary.

Be careful not to harp on the awful consequences that bankruptcy will bring upon you and your family for that suggests that your arm is being twisted. But make it clear that your situation is rather grave. A certain bet of humour at your expense will lighten the tone of the letter.

Dear Nikhil,

I am sorry I have not kept in touch with you for some time, but I hope our parents are keeping well. It was nice to hear their voices over the telephone last week. They both sounded very cheerful.

I am sorry to say that I have got myself into a mess, and I need your help. My business has suddenly taken a nose-dive, and I owe my friend, from whom I had taken a temporary loan, Rs. 5,000. He wants it urgently to pay for his daughter's school fees, and right now I am unable to rustle up that amount immediately.

I don't like to ask you for money, but I don't like to ask anyone else either. As I said, the immediate problem is Rs. 5,000, and I hope you can send me this amount at once. I shall of course pay back with interest as soon as it is possible.

I trust Madhu and Madhav are studying well. Please give them our best wishes, and regards to our parents and my dear sister-in-law.

Your loving brother,
Nandan

12

INVITATIONS AND ANNOUNCEMENTS

When sending out invitations and announcements, certain rules of etiquette have to be followed. In days gone by, these seemed quite straightforward as you followed the prescribed formulas. Or else society would look at you with disdain and disapproval.

Now a days things are neither so simple nor so risky. People are no longer formal, and so also are some invitations and announcements so impersonal as to be downright rude. But they have to be taken care of when you are sending out invitations and announcements on various special occasions.

SPECIAL OCCASIONS

People all over the world like to celebrate special occasions like weddings, births, engagements, etc. They can be formal, informal, or elaborate rituals. These are occasions when people gather in large numbers in their best dresses; there is plenty to eat and drink, there is music and dancing, etc. All of us like to make the day special.

These days there are some modern-minded people who shun ceremonies that seem stuffy or artificial. It then becomes very difficult to strike a balance between the solemn or formal side of the occasion and the personal joy behind it.

It is, as a rule, for the hosts to decide exactly what course to take. Whether it is a wedding or a baby-naming ceremony, or even a funeral, all the arrangements should be left to the family organising it.

Remember, what may appeal to your closest friends and immediate family may be looked down upon disapprovingly by straitlaced people, old-fashioned aunts or crusty grandfathers.

SENDING AND ANSWERING

Following the prescribed patterns when it comes to sending out formal invitations is convenient.

When you have to invite people to a party, a wedding, a graduation, etc., a lot of organisation is required. The guests have to be informed well in advance so that you know how many will be attending the function. You may hardly find the time to write personal letters to all, so send them printed invitations.

You can reserve handwritten letters along with the printed invitations for the most special of the guests, the immediate family members.

Any invitations you receive should be answered promptly, within two or three days. It is extremely bad manners not to reply. When someone has taken the trouble to invite you, you must let them know whether you are able to accept, and the sooner the better.

So when you receive announcements of a birth/death/change of address/engagement, etc. It would be courteous on your part to acknowledge receipt and to offer your congratulations or commiserations as the occasion demands. The sender will be assured that the invitation has been received.

FORMAL INVITATIONS AND ANNOUNCEMENTS

Formal invitations have a fixed format. They may be handwritten or printed, but never on business letterhead stationery. The invitation is centred on the paper. Generally, it is not necessary to send formal invitations to family and close friends for dinner parties, social gatherings, etc.

Keep the invitation plain and simple, avoiding gaudiness, silly design, irrelevant details, striking colours, and a general tone of sentimentality. Profuse expressions of sorrow or sympathy should be confined to personal letters.

Avoid typing invitations or announcements, or even replies. They are best suited for business matters or even for personal letters. But formal invitations or announcements should be handwritten, or printed cards sent.

RULES FOR ALL FORMAL NOTICES

The following are accepted rules for all types of formal invitation:

1) Use plain white, cream or ivory card. You can have some permissible edging such as gilding, but keep the decoration simple. For announcements of deaths and invitations to funerals and rituals, a black band around the margins is normal.

2) Use good quality paper for handwritten invitations. It can be white or off-white. You can also use your own headed notepaper. For semi-formal occasions, you can use general-purpose cards,

3) The printing on all formal invitations is usually black. You can use gold too, but it may look gaudy. Use black ink if you are writing cards or letters by hand.

4) Always write in the third person:

   Mr. & Mrs. Sharma

   Request the pleasure ......

5) Don't use abbreviations, such as Mon., Capt., Hon'ble, etc. You, as hosts, may abbreviate your own titles if you wish:

   Dr. & Mrs Makhija

   Try to give the full form of dates and times:

   Monday, 14 june, 1999 at 6 p.m.

Some write out even these in full:

Monday, the Fourteenth of June 1999

At 6 o'clock in the evening

6) Centre the lines of the text, leaving the name of the addressee at the top left, the return address where relevant, the reason for the function, the reply instructions such as RSVP or Regrets Only. The last two are usually set at the bottom left corner.

Mr. & Mrs. Sengupta
Request the pleasure of your company
at a luncheon to
celebrate the birth of their son
at our residence
Palmgrove Residency
34, M.G. Road, Bangalore-1
on Friday, 10 January 2000
at 12:30 p.m.

RSVP
Pradeep
Tel. No. 4222071

7) Avoid using punctuation at the end of each line. Punctuation has to be used only when words have to be separated within a line.

The following information should be included in all invitations:

a) The name of the person sponsoring the event—the host/hostess.

b) The name of the recipients.

c) The nature of the social event, and usually the occasion for it.

d) The address where the function is to take place.

e) The date and time of the function, in that order.

f) The address for replies, if this differs from the address of the function, and the contact phone number.

g) Directions or a simple map if the location may be difficult to find.

Always use full names when sending or replying to formal invitations. Generally, a wife's first name is omitted if she is clubbed together with her husband.

Mr. and Mrs. Yogender Sharma

ENGAGEMENTS

In the olden days it was not uncommon that a girl's parents to choose the man she was going to marry. Since then things have changed, though in India the system still prevails widely.

There are three ways of formally announcing an engagement:

1) by note
2) at an engagement party
3) through the newspapers

Your immediate family can be informed over the phone, or face to face. You can inform your distant family members and friends through your handwritten letter. The letter can be short and simple.

If you plan to hold a formal engagement party, the invitation can be any type of normal notice.

Mr. & Mrs Ashwin Madappa
Request the pleasure of the company of
Mr. & Mrs. Vasu Chingappa
At the engagement party
of their daughter Reshma
with Sunil Somanna
at

The Country Club
Jayanagar, Bangalore-70
on Saturday, 2 October 1990
at 4 p.m.

RSVP
Preeth
Tel. No. 26663313

The letter that you write, with which you may enclose the invitation card, should be warm and very informal, and share your personal feelings about the event, especially while writing to very close family members. At most times, the announcement of an engagement is done through an invitation card, as shown above, and this card need not have an accompanying letter when inviting friends or distant relatives.

If you want to announce an engagement in a newspaper, the editorial staff can guide you on the wording. Be sure though that your family hears the news before it appears in the press.

You must first choose the newspaper in which you want the engagement announcement to appear. You will probably send it to your local and city newspapers. There is more of a chance that your announcement will apppear in a local newspaper, but it does not hurt to try to have your announcement appear in a larger city newspaper. Once this has been decided, contact the papers to find out whether they publish engagement announcements.

In addition, you should find out the following information:

1) To whom should you send the enagagement announcement at the newspaper office?
2) Does the newspaper accept photos? If so, are there specific size requirements?
3) How long after the editor receives the engagement announcement will it before the announcement appears in the paper?

4) Is there a specific format you should use when preparing your announcements?

Once you have these answers, begin to prepare your announcement in the newspaper. Be as brief and to the point as posssible. Include a release date when the announcement should appear. Also include a contact name and telephone number in case the editor needs to contact you to verify information. If you are including a photograph, make sure it is black, white and glossy. Engagement photos are generally a head and shoulders shot of the couple. Do not be surprised if your announcement does not appear exactly word for word the way you wrote it. It is a standard practice for the editor to rework press announcements.

Example

> *Mr. & Mrs. S. Dhareshwar of Navi Mumbai announce the engagement of their son, Sachin,to Jyotika, the daughter of Mr. & Mrs. S. Satwalekar of Greenacres, Madukari.*

When you get news of your friends engagement you should write your congratulations immediately. Such a letter calls for a reply in turn, and you can furnish any details about the marriage if you want to.

WEDDINGS

Invitations set the tone for your wedding as well as inform guests of the date, place and hosts of the celebration. Invitations should be mailed six to eight weeks before the wedding date so as to give your guests plenty of time to make the necessary arrangements to attend the wedding, and also to reply.

Wedding invitations are traditionally printed on a white paper. To give a very personal touch to very close members of the family and very close friends, you can enclose a personal letter inviting them to attend and grace the occasion. If you are inviting the whole family, you can address it as :

Mr. & Mrs. Gulab Singh and Family

Example of a Wedding Invitation Card

Mr. & Mrs. Jacob Thomas
request the pleasure of your company
at the marriage of their daughter
Jennifer
to
Major Wilson Craig
at St. Philomena's Church,
2 Bank Street, Trichy
on Sunday, 19 August 1999
at 11 a.m.

RSVP
2, Railway Quarters, Trichy -7

Colonel & Mrs. S. Narayanan
request the pleasure of your company
at the marriage of their son
Balaji
to
Shanta
at Barat Ghar, Sarojini Nagar, New Delhi
on Monday, 2 February 1995
at 10 a.m.
Wedding ceremony : 10-11.30 a.m.
Lunch: 1 p.m

Wedding announcements share the news of your marriage with those who are unable to attend your marriage. The ceremony might be taking place abroad, or it might be a simple registered marriage where only your nearest relatives are invited. In such cases, the thing to send is a wedding announcement rather than a wedding invitation.

The following are a few guidelines that will be useful for writing invitations:

1) State the occasion, date, time and place.
2) Include addresses and a map of the place where the wedding is to be held.
3) Mention the timing of the marriage, lunch, reception, dinner.
4) Include a telephone number for RSVPs.
5) Express that you are looking forward to seeing the person.
6) If you do not want gifts, briefly state that gifts are not wanted, or simply state 'no gifts please'. Explain that their presence is the only gift you need.
7) Make sure you send out your invitations well in advance.

If you plan to make announcement of your wedding in a newspaper, ring the paper at least two weeks before the wedding. You may want the wedding itself to be reported. The newspaper staff may send a reporter and photographer to the wedding.

If, for certain reasons, the wedding is postponed, you should use the telephone to inform guests of any change of plans.

DEATHS

When a death in the family occurs, you will want to announce it to your closest family and friends around you, as soon as possible.

After this, you should send an announcement of the death to the newspaper that you want to insert it in.

A death notice usually includes the date and place of death, the names of the funeral or ceremonial rituals .

S. Hemant, Asst.Secy (Retd.), Zonal Office, LIC of India, attained Lord's Lotus feet on June 5, 1998 at 6:40 a.m. Final obsequies will be held on June 6, at No-2, Valmiki Road, Koramangala, Bangalore-20. Ph. (080)5213924

Budy Michael died on 18 September 1990 at Apollo Hospital, New Delhi. Mourned by beloved husband Dan, children Stella and Simon. Funeral Saturday, 11 a.m at Sacred Hearts Church, Lajpat Nagar.

BIRTHS

The birth of a baby in a family is usually a happy occasion.

The announcement of the birth can be made amongst relatives and close friends by telephone. Letters and cards can be sent out to the others.

Extend an invitation to the naming ceremony of the baby. The tone of the invitation should be positive in anticipation of the joyous occasion. State clearly the date, time, address, and details like lunch or tea or dinner.

If you are making an announcement of the birth of the baby in a newspaper your notice should look something like the following:

This is to announce the birth of Rishab on July 10 at Pant Hospital, Jamshedpur, to Mayura, the wife of Captain Alok Jain.

When you receive the news of the birth of the baby, you should respond immediately. Letters, cards and flowers can be sent or taken personally to the mother at the hospital. If you live in another city, you can send a pretty congratulatory card, possibly with a letter to give that personal touch.

ANNIVERSARIES

Wedding anniversaries are celebrated all over the world, but four special ones are silver (25 years), ruby (40 years), golden (50 years), and diamond (60 years).

There are no fixed ways of celebrating each anniversary. Some like to go out for dinner, some host parties, some may go out of the city for a few days. If you know someone has a wedding anniversary, you can send them a card and some flowers, or you can at least greet them over the telephone.

OFFICIAL FUNCTIONS

When you are working for a company, you may have to send out invitations to public functions. The invitations are somewhat similar to those of weddings. The invitations are normally printed on white paper.

Official functions are held for various purposes: "to mark the hundredth anniversary of ....", "for the opening of ...." or "for the presentation of awards by..."

Invitations to official functions often give the time of the function and the time by which guests are supposed to be seated

At the head of the invitation, name any guests of honour.

The Board of Directors
request the honour of the presence of
Mr. & Mrs. Nitin Desai
at the inauguration of
Infosys, Mysore
on February 12, 2005 at 12 noon
Dr. Manmohan Singh, Hon'ble Prime Minister
will inaugurate the campus.
Mr. T.N. Chaturvedi, Hon'ble Governor
will preside over the function.
Venue
The Amphitheatre, Infosys Technologies Ltd.
Hootagalli, Mysore 571186
(You are requested to be seated by 11.30 a.m.)

If you want to have limited people attending the function you might add the words, 'Please' bring this card with you, at the bottom.

INFORMAL INVITATIONS

When you want to send invitations for less formal occasions, a short handwritten note or telephone call is enough. In an informal letter of invitation, use the first person or second person (I, we, you) rather than the third person (he, she, they).

You can send informal invitations on correspondence cards that are the size and shape of a postcard, with the name, address and telephone number of the sender printed along the long top edge.

Example of a short note

Dear Mr. & Mrs. Bajaj,

We would be happy if you could come with the children to our place around 7.00 p.m. We are having a fireworks party with a bar-be-cue and drinks. Please let us know by phone.

Yours

Bela Singh

Example of an informal card

DR. & MRS. M. PATIL

Dinner, Friday 3rd May

Please confirm by phone 8.00 P.M.

Example of a correspondence card

Mr. & Mrs. Sahay, 2 Oakton Apts., R.V.Nagar, Jaipur-2

Madhu & Sunil

Drinks, Saturday 5th June, 7.30 p.m.

Regrets only

REPLIES

It is very important to reply when you receive any invitations. How you accept or decline an invitation depends on the type of invitation you have received. It is always better to send replies handwritten.

Generally, if the invitation is a formal one, the reply should match. If the tone and wording of the reply reflect that of the invitation, so replying should not be a hurdle. If your reply is a

PART II
BUSINESS LETTERS

13

THE BASICS

A business letter is more formal than a personal letter. Millions of us write letters as part of our work, but few of us know the keys to an effective business letter. Too many business letters are impersonal, long-winded and difficult or tedious to read.

Most writers hide behind tired phrases and an over-formal approach when writing business letters. When you write a letter you create an image of you and your company in your readers mind. A good letter should be effortless reading that makes you want to read more. It should be clear and concise, with short sentences and simple words. It should keep to the facts, and be easy to read and to understand.

THE SEVEN CS OF BUSINESS LETTER WRITING

Effective letter writing boils down to knowing why you are writing a letter, understanding your reader's needs and then clearly writing what you need to say.

Every letter should be clear, helpful and as friendly as the topic allows. The best letters have a conversational tone and read as if you were talking to your reader.

The seven Cs of letter writing are: clear, concise, correct, courteous, conversational, convincing, complete.

When you write a letter, you are trying to convince someone to act or react in a positive way. Show you are interested in the reader's circumstances. If he mentions something personal in the letter refer to it in your reply. This builds a bridge between you and the reader. Read the original letter carefully and see if there is something you can put in your letter to show your interest.

PUTTING YOUR READER FIRST

For all writers the most important people are their readers. They want relevant information presented in a clear, easy-to-understand style. They want to get the gist of your message in one reading, so avoid long sentences and boring style. You will have to adapt your style and content to meet their needs.

KEEPING YOUR BUSINESS PLAN TO THE POINT

The first step in any writing task is to set down your aim. The clearer you are in your mind about what you want to achieve, the better will be your letter. It will help you focus on the information that supports your central aim, and to cut out information that is irrelevant. You can write the clearest letter, but if it does not say anything worth knowing, it is a useful document. The more specific information you give, the better. You must be ruthless in cutting out the padding most of us put into letters.

To help you keep to the point of your letter, you can draw up an outline to plan your letter.

1) Make a list of the topics you want to cover, but don't worry about the order.

2) Under each topic, list key words, examples, arguments and facts.

3) Review each topic in your outline for relevance to your aim and audience.

4) Cut out anything that is not relevant.

5) Sort out the information into the best order.

You don't have to stick rigidly to your business letter plan as it may change if you discover new information. By breaking down a complex topic into subject areas, you will find it easier to concentrate on the most relevant information.

SETTING THE RIGHT TONE TO THE LETTER

When you write a business letter, it is important to use a tone that is friendly but efficient. To do this, write as you would speak and talk, on paper. This does not mean that you should use slang or bad grammar, but try to aim for a conversational style.

Use contractions such as: it's, doesn't , you're, we're, isn't, don't, which will give a personal and human feel to your writing. You don't have to use contractions at every opportunity. Sometimes, writing 'do not' comes more naturally than 'don't'.

Use personal references such as I, we, you, your, my and our in your writing. This helps you to avoid using passive verbs. It makes your style more direct and clear. So instead of writing, "Our address records have been amended...", write, "We've changed your address in our records..."

Use direct questions which are an essential part of the spoken language. Using them gives your writing much more impact, and as a common technique in marketing and advertising material.

Write your business letter in plain English. Good writing is effortless reading that makes you want to read more. It is clear and concise, uses short sentences and simple words. It keeps the fact, and is easy to read and understand.

Plain English is simple and direct, but not simplistic or patronising. Use active verbs rather than passive ones, as they make you writing simpler, less formal, clearer and more precise. In oustead of saying, "It was agreed by the committee…", write, " The committee agreed…"

Keep your sentence length low. The length is crucial to good writing. Almost everything written by good writers has an average sentence length of 15-20 words. You can vary the length and rhythm—balance long and short sentences, but keep the average length well below 20 words.

Use simple words rather than complex ones. Simple, everyday words will help you to get your message across. Instead of 'additional' , you can use 'extra' , 'indicate'—'show', 'initiate'—'start', 'proliferate'—'spread'.

Economy of words is the mark of good writing. You must edit ruthlessly, cutting any irrelevant word.

For examples

Use	*instead of*
Later	*at a later date*
Now	*at the present time*
For	*for the purpose of*
Besides	*in addition to*
Regularly	*on a regular basis*

Avoid using jargon and technical terms. Also avoid using abbreviations. The most common and irritating form of jargon is overuse of abbreviations.

Avoid abstract words and phrases like amenities, devices, processes, variables, etc.

A business letter should have a margin of at least an inch on all four edges. There are six parts to business letter:

The Heading

This contains the return address (usually two or three lines) with the date on the last line. Sometimes it may be necessary to include a line after the address and before the date, for a phone number, fax number, e-mail address, or something similar. Often a line is skipped between the address and the date. It is not necessary to type the return address if you are using stationery with the return address already imprinted. Always include the date.

Example

Alpha Books Limited
25, Mahatma Gandhi Road
Bangalore-560002
Ph.: 080-26667626 Fax: 91-80- 26667628
Email : alphabooks@touchtelindia.net
24 June 1985

The Inside Address

This is the address you are sending your letter to. Make it as complete as possible. Include titles and names if you know them. This is always on the left margin. If a paper is folded in thirds to fit in a standard 9-inch business envelope, the inside address can appear through the window in the envelope. An inside address also helps the recipient route the letter properly, and can help should the envelope be damaged and the address become unreadable. Skip a line after the heading before the inside address, skip another line after the inside address and before the greeting.

In case the letter is confidential write it just above the inside address in capital letters.

Example

CONFIDENTIAL
Messrs. Agarwal Packers
2, Ansari Road
Daryagunj
New Delhi - 110002

Attention Line

This is a line which carries the name of the individual for whom the letter is intended.

ATTENTION: MR. PAUL JOSEPH, SUPPLY DEPARTMENT

This inclusion enables the receiving company to hand it over to the right person without delay or confusion. This line is generally given when the letter is addressed to a company or organisation but you want it specifically to be handled by a particular individual.

The Greeting

This line is also called the salutation. The greeting in a business letter is always formal. It normally begins with the word 'Dear' and always includes the person's last name. It normally has a title. Use a first name only if the title is unclear, for example, you are writing to someone named 'Suman', but do not know whether the person is male or female.

The greeting starts with a capital letter and ends with a comma.

The salutation is written on the upper left-hand side just below the heading while in some countries it is common to have the name of the person, to whom the letter is being sent, in the salutation. In India, the salutation 'Dear Sir' or 'Dear Sirs' is the most frequently used form. For strictly formal occasions 'Sir' or 'Sirs' is used, while 'Gentlemen' is normally used when writing to professional firms.

The Subject

This is an important part of a business letter that should not be avoided, as it gives a clear indication of the purpose of the letter. You have to write a powerful subject heading for your letter. Can you imagine reading a newspaper or magazine without any headlines or headings? Writing good headings or subjects transform your business letter, and organise the information to help your reader.

Example

Subject: Madekeri Land Deal

If some reference has been given in a previous letter received, you may quote it.

Reference: Your letter no. GF 215/92 dated June, 1992

The Body

The body is written as text. A business letter is never handwritten. Depending on the letter style you choose, paragraphs may be indented. Regardless of the format, skip a line between paragraphs, skip a line between the body and the close.

Your first job in writing any letter is to gain your reader's attention. It is an important principle of effective writing to put the most important information first. Your opening paragraph is both the headline and the lead for the message that follows in the rest of the letter. Don't weigh down the front of your letter with boring repetition of information that your reader already knows. Many letters fail to start well because they follow the standard paragraph of every business letter. The following are some typical examples of openings in business letters:

a) Thank you for your letter of 8 March 1998, which has been passed to me for my attention.

b) I refer to previous correspondence in respect of the above, and note that to date we have not received your cheque for the outstanding arrears.

c) I write with reference to our telephone conversation yesterday regarding the above matter.

Starting with a reference to the incoming letter is weak and wastes your reader's time. Most readers skip it, looking to the second and third paragraphs to get the answer to their questions. So get rid of any opening reference to the reader's letter and answer the most important question, or give the most relevant information in your first sentence.

The various topics should be written down in order of their significance. Devote a paragraph to each topic.

The Complementary Close

This short, polite closing ends with a comma. Also known as subscription, it is either at the left margin or its left edge is in the centre, depending on the style you use. It begins at the same column as the heading does. The block style is becoming more widely used because there is no indenting to bother with in the whole letter. Normally, you skip three lines after the body to write the subscription.

The Signature Line

Skip two lines and type out the name to be signed. This includes a middle initial but does not have to. Women may indicate how they wish to be addressed by placing Miss , Mrs., Ms., Dr., or similar title in parentheses before their name. The signature line may include a second line for a title of appropriate. The signature should start directly above the first letter of the signature line in the space between the close and the signature line. Use blue or black ink. Business letters should not contain postscripts.

Enclosures

If you are enclosing a paper, document, etc., with the letter, write about it at the bottom left-hand corner of the letter.

Example

Encls: Two

Superscription

This deals with the recipient's address on the envelope. Write the full name and address on it carefully and legibly.

The top or bottom left corner of the envelope should carry your full name and address.

Some business letters can be very long, especially when you have to include the job title and department. You can combine elements on one line as long as this causes no confusion.

Sample Business Letter

Barton & Sons Ltd.

2, Mahatma Gandhi Road, Bangalore-2

Tel: 080-22513161 Fax: 080 - 22513393

Ref: SM/wk/102 *9 October, 1990*

Mr. Rajiv Seth
Marketing Director
Swale Wines Ltd.
22, Sahji Road, Banjara
Hyderubud- 500002

Dear Mr. Seth,

Subject: *Proposed Joint Marketing Strategy*

We are writing in answer to your letter of 25 September 1990, having given the points you raise due consideration. You asked that our company set up a joint approach in marketing with yours, and we are now able to tell you what we have decided.

The board has concluded that the scheme you suggest would not justify itself in the medium to long term.

We therefore feel that we cannot for the time being see any way that your proposals could be put profitably into effect, but we shall inform you if at any stage this position changes.

Yours sincerely
David Barton
Managing Director

14

ENQUIRIES AND REQUESTS

Public organisations and companies are usually ready to supply all sorts of information as this will be good publicity for them.

Five basic rules have to be followed for all letters of enquiry:

1) Use a separate line or paragraph for each item of information that you want.
2) Do not bother to inform them why you need the information, unless you are asking for confidential information.
3) State in the opening sentence what the subject of your enquiry is.
4) Avoid being demanding or ingratiating. Don't use phrases such as, " I'm sorry to take up your valuable time".
5) Thank them in advance. This is a sure way to get a response. If you have asked for something unusual and get what you want, write a thank you note, acknowledging receipt.

A Polite Request

When something has gone with a product, write a polite letter to the manufacturers that will get you their cooperation.

Example

Kishore Sahu
2, Langdon Road,

Cox Town,
Bangalore
10 March, 1991

M/s Prescott Toys Co. Ltd.
12 Jharsa Road
Sector 15
Gurgaon - 120002.

Dear Sirs,

***Sub:** Request for Spare parts*

Your company is reputed for good quality toys, and also for service. So I have no hesitation in writing to you now.

Two years ago I had purchased your electronic soccer game. It has been very frequently used. The other day a welded joint snapped, and our son cannot use it with repairing it.

Is it possible to return the game to you for rewelding ? My son and I would be very grateful if it could be repaired.

Yours sincerely

Roshan Malhotra

Writing to Authorities

While writing to the authorities, you need to be polite as well as very concise.

Example

Dear Sir,

***Sub.:** Loss of Driving Licence*

My car, a grey Maruti 800, registration MH 6420, was recently broken into. Among the things stolen were papers relating to the car, including my driving licence.

Please issue a duplicate licence.

Yours faithfully
Prateek Chaudhury

Request for a Catalogue

4 November, 1990

Messrs. Ramesh Publishing House

Navneet Nagar

Sagar

Dear Sirs,

Sub.: *Request for Catalogue*

We are interested in bulk purchase of your books for our school library.

Please send us a catalogue of your books.

Also let us know how much discount you extend to schools.

Yours faithfully

Reply to the Letter

15 November,1990

Bharati Girls Higher Secondary School

Bapuji Nagar,

Sagar

Dear Madam,

Thank you for your letter of 4 November 1980.

Enclosed please find our detailed catalogue of books published for schools.

We give 25 per cent discount to all schools.

We look forward to your order.

Yours faithfully

Enquiry About Television Sets

Apurva Traders

2, Lala Lajpat Marg,

Kanpur

5 April, 1999

M/s. Pankaj Electronics
Green Park Main Road,
New Delhi -110016

Sir,

Subject: *Purchase of TV sets*

We would like to purchase five sets each of Akai, Onida and LG television for our Delhi branch shop.

Please inform us the discount you will allow on each set, and other incentives if we place more bulk orders for the sets.

Please treat this as most urgent.

Yours faithfully,

Reply to the Letter

Pankaj Electronics
Green Park Main Rd,
New Delhi-16
15 April, 1999

Apurva Traders
2, Lala Lajpaat Marg,
Kanpur

Dear Sir,

Thank you for your enquiry about the bulk purchase of television sets.

We are glad to offer you 10 per cent discount on Akai, Onida and LG sets.

In case you are planning to purchase in bulk, we shall offer you 15 per cent.

We look forward to your orders.

Yours faithfully,

DEALING WITH REPLIES

Most people receive enquiries through the post-enquiries about their financial standing, their work and interests, requests for information about some piece of business, or enquiries from the bank on some matter related to a loan.

Some letters need to be dealt with promptly, accurately and politely. It is in your own interests to do so quickly and smoothly if you want responses with comparable efficiency.

Replies are simpler to write than enquiries. Tackle questions one by one in turn, preferably on separate lines. You can number them, but make sure that your numbers correspond to those of the questions you are answering.

CONFIRMATIONS AND ACKNOWLEDGEMENTS

Most replies can be very short. A typical reply includes acknowledgement of receipt.

Example

Dear Mr. Manek,

I acknowledge receipt of your letter of 15 June. I shall answer the questions you raise when I hear from my bank.

Yours sincerely,

Similarly letters confirming details are straightforward.

Example

Dear Mr Nandan

Your ref. Ad315

Thank you for your letter of 2 January regarding the booking of our holiday in Austria.

I confirm that the answers to your queries 1-3 and 5-6 are all yes.

Concerning point 4, please note that we do not prefer to travel by night, unless it is the only option for April 10.

Will you now please go ahead with the final booking and confirm as soon as possible that these have been made.

Yours sincerely,

COMPLAINTS, CLAIMS AND ADJUSTMENTS

Many times you hear of people getting a raw deal with a defective car, or a stereo system that comes with some essential component missing, or some other similar problem. Don't hesitate or feel shy about complaining. Good shops and manufacturers welcome feedback from customers, and will do their best to help. They would like to know about defects in their goods. And if the dealers are not good, it is your duty to yourself and to others to see that they do not get away with it.

Sometimes there are inordinate delays in receiving goods. Sometimes goods are damaged, at other times there is some variance in the quantity or quality of goods in the terms and conditions of the payment and delivery of the goods offered. Care should be taken while drafting such letters. Be polite, avoid offensive language and exaggerated statements.

Adjustment letters are replies to the complaints, skilfully drafted to appease and satisfy the customer as well as to protect your own business. After checking and investigating the complaint, a courteous reply should be sent immediately to the customer informing him that an investigation is being made, and you would get back to him soon.

Avoid using such phrases as, "surprise" "disappointment", "errors are bound to happen", "it is the first time such a thing has happened", "it could not be avoided", "we hope this kind of trouble will not occur in future".

Don't forget, if your complaint receives satisfactory treatment, to write a note of thanks to the company.

Sometimes, you are left wondering as to whom you should complain to. If your new washing machine stops functioning the moment you start using it, the first thing to do is to look at the papers that come with it, especially the guarantee card. You can then complain to the dealer who sold you the product.

If it is a service that you want to complain about, go to the provider of the service—the telephone company, the gas agency, the travel agent, etc. Write a letter to them about your complaint.

The tone and approach of your letter must be right. Your letter is more likely to work if you sound hurt rather than outraged, if you assume that it is probably an oversight rather than bloody-minded inefficiency.

A letter of complaint should include the following:

1) Any reference number that the company has given you.
2) A detailed description of the product—brand, model, serial or identification number, size, colour, price, and the like.
3) Place of purchase, together with the name and address of the retailer.
4) Date of purchase.
5) Copies of the relevant documents—not the originals.
6) A short description of the problem sifting the main formats from incidental details.
7) A clear statement of what you expect the company to do for you—to refund the purchase cost, for example, to compensate you for your trouble, to provide free servicing, or to replace the defective article.

Example : Goods Damaged in Transit

Greenways Club
Upper Golf Links,
Ooty -5

Kalyani Breweries
Ammaguda Terminus,

Secunderabad

Dear Sirs,

Sub. : *Our order GC/101 dated 15 January 2001*

We regret to inform you that a whole crate of beer bottles reached us in a broken condition. The beer had spilt all over the crate.

Kindly replace the crate of beer bottles to compensate for the loss we suffered.

We expect you to act immediately and send us a reply promptly

Yours faithfully,

Example of Non-Delivery of Goods

2, V Main, XI Cross,
Malleswaram
Bangalore -3
10 August 2000

Sudha Book House
2, Richmond Road,
Royapettah
Chennai

Dear Sirs,

Sub.: *Non-delivery of books*

It is more than a month since I placed orders with you for the supply of 30 books. Though you acknowledged the order on 20 August, I have not yet received the books.

As I had mentioned in my letter, these books are needed urgently.

Please dispatch them immediately failing which I may have to cancel the order.

Yours faithfully

Reply to the above

Sudha Book House
2,Richmond Road,
Royapettah,
Chennai -2
13 August, 2000

Dear Sir,

Thank you for your letter dated 10 August 2000. We are sorry for the inconvenience caused to you.

Today we are dispatching the books that you have ordered by courier.

We once again apologies for the delay.

Yours faithfully,

Example: Letter to a Car Dealer

2, Cunningham Road,
Bangalore-2
22 July 2002

Ashok and Sons Limited
Gandhi Bazaar,
Bangalore - 20

Dear Sirs,

Sub.: Demand for services

Ref: 435/rd

In June this year I bought from you a red WagonR car, year of manufacture 2001, licence number KA4253, price Rs. 4,00,000.

Since then, every time I have driven the vehicle another fault has come to light. I enclose a copy of a report made by my garage, vani Vilas Garage, which lists 19 major faults. You will note that they also suspect that the mileometer has been tampered with.

I have discussed this matter with you over the telephone on several occasions. I have also written to you letters on June 25 and 2 July, none of which I have received replies to.

I am very dissatisfied with the vehicle and your after sales service. I expect your reply to this letter before July end, either:

1. *offering to correct all the listed faults or*
2. *refunding the full purchase price.*

Enclosed you will find copies of:

a) *the report made by Vani Vilas Garage*

b) *your sales certificate*

c) *your receipt for the purchase of the vehicle*

d) *the registration document*

e) *your guarantee*

I look forward to receiving your reply. Failure to respond to this lettter will result in my going to consumer court with a view to initiating steps to recoup my losses.

Yours faithfully,

Examples—Refusal to accept goods.

15 October, 2000

Dear Sir,

Yesterday I received the six boxes of chocolate from you.

I regret to say that the chocolates do not conform to the specifications that I had mentioned. I had specified that the chocolates had to be dark and sweet, made of cocoa, but instead you have sent me white milk chocolates.

I am extremely sorry to return these, but shall be glad if you substitute these for dark chocolates as early as possible.

Yours faithfully,

Example—Claiming Allowance

2 December, 2000

Dear Sirs,

This morning one of my customers returned five boxes of chocolate to me saying that they had worms in them, and hence unfit for consumption.

This is an unfortunate occurrence, especially as your chocolates were on a trial order. I suggest that you give me credit for their value which may be deducted from my future payments to you.

Yours truly,

Example—Asking for a Credit Note

24 February, 2000

Satyam Publishers
Ramana Street,
S N Nagar
Jhanjarur- 5

Dear Sirs,

Thank you for your letter dated 15 February 2000.

Accordingly, we are returning today the following books by registered post:

1. *Buddhism - Zen Philosophy —10 copies*
2. *Strange Philosophies —15 copies*
3. *Creating a Void —25 copies.*

Please issue us a credit note against the return of the above books to be adjusted against the next order.

Thanking you,

Your faithfully,

Example—Adjustment Letter

5 November, 2000

Dear Mr. Sitaram,

We have dispatched today by courier to you a new set of cassettes and compact discs,

We regret very much that the cassettes and compact discs reached you in a damaged condition. This time we have taken care by way of providing extra cushioning to avoid any possibility of scratches and damage.

Please return the damaged cassettes and compact discs by parcel post addressed with the enclosed label. A damage report, filled out according to the facts described in your letter, is also enclosed. Please sign and return it in the business reply envelope for our insurance record.

Yours very truly,

____

15

DAY-TO-DAY TRADING

Day-to-day trading involves letters that you have to write in the course of everyday business—covering letters, estimates, invoices, letters informing clients of price increases, answering customer's enquiries, and so on.

COVERING LETTERS

You should always enclose a covering letter when you send samples or documents. In that letter say exactly what you are sending and give any explanations that you think will help. Always ask for an acknowledgement.

1 November 2000

Dear Mr. Mahadev,

I enclose the Builder's Report, and various other documents relating to the property at 7, Ashoka Road, Mysore.

The documents are:

1. *Builder's Report*
2. *Karnataka State Valuation Report*
3. *Copies (3) of documents relating to the property*

Kindly acknouledge safe receipt.

We await your further instructions in this matter.

Yours sincerely,

ESTIMATES QUOTATIONS AND TENDERS

An estimate or quotation offers specific services or goods to a potential client at a certain price.

The difference between the two is that, while an estimate may be amended at a later date, a quotation is legally binding if accepted.

An offer is made to accelerate the pace of sales. It is meant for both existing as well as prospective customers. A voluntary offer is targetted to boost the sales of a business house.

A quotation, also with the aim of boosting the sales of a business house, is in response to an enquiry made by a business house or a person.

An estimate refers to rendering of services against a particular price. A tender is an offer that is usually submitted in response to an advertisement.

Estimates and quotations are usually made on standard forms, though you can use ordinary letter paper. Remember to include the following items (as well, of course, as the usual letterhead information—address, telephone number, date, and so on):

1) a reference number, plus any reference number that the prospective customer requires.
2) full details of the goods or services.
3) the price per unit, and where applicable, the price of the required quantity.
4) all other fees or charges, including carriage.
5) your terms and conditions of payment.
6) the initials 'E&OE' standing for Errors and Omissions Excepted', a safeguard reminding the receiver that the price may be different if something has been overlooked, or if a mistake has been plainly made.

Producers or manufacturers make offers of their products to retailers, offering incentives like discounts or concessions. While making offers, your approach should be particularly courteous and carefully worded.

Example—Offer of Leather Shoes

Kalpana Traders
2 Moti Bagh,
Talgaon -1
24 April 2000

Shoeworld
Agra Cantt
Agra -2

Dear Sirs,

Subject : *Offer of Leather Shoes*

We have received the latest sets of leather shoes that are in fashion today. We are enclosing a catalogue of the varieties in style, colour, etc. including the price of each pair of shoes.

The prices are competitively low right now, and are expected to rise in a couple of months.

We hope that you place your orders as early as possible to avail of the low prices.

Yours faithfully,

Example—Offer of Tea

Prospect Tea Company
The Nilgiries,
5 July 2001

The Manager,
Bharat Tea Traders,
Ramnagar
Coimbatore -9

Dear Sirs,

Subject : *Offer of Orange Pekoe Tea*

We are happy to inform you that we have slashed down the tea prices in South India. We have large stocks of tea–orange pekoe–

with us. We are enclosing a list of tea and its varieties, and the discount against each that we are offering.

We hope these specific incentives will tempt you to place your orders with us as early as possible.

Yours faithfully,

An estimate is not legally binding on the person submitting it. He can withdraw it before it is accepted.

Example—Estimate for Carpeting a Room

Mayura Hotel
Rajaji Marg,
Aurangabad
2 September 2000

Shaman Carpets House
Upper Mall,
Shimla,

Dear Sirs,

We are planning at recarpet all the rooms in our hotel.

The following rooms need to be carpeted:

1) *double rooms (20), each measuring—20 ft × 20 ft*
2) *suites (4), Each measuring—*
   bedroom 15 ft × 15ft,
   sitting room 15 ft × 15 ft
3) *reception area, measuring—40 ft × 20 ft*
4) *lounge, measuring—40 ft × 40 ft*
5) *dining room, measuring—50 ft × 50 ft*
6) *conference room, measuring—80 ft × 50 ft*
7) *corridors (4), measuring—120ft × 50 ft*

Kindly give us an estimate of the cost for carpeting all these areas.

We would also appreciate if you could send us a catalogue of your carpet designs and colours.

An immediate response will be highly appreciated.

Thanking you,

Yours faithfully,

Quotations must include the quality and quantity of goods offered, the terms of payment, the mode of delivery, cash or credit, packaging and handling charges, and so on.

Example—Quotation for Training Course

C Dot Computers
32, 11th Cross,
Banjara hills,
Hyderabad
15 May 2000

Padma Secretarial School
15, Sikh Village
Trimulgherry
Secunderabad

Dear sirs

Subject: *Quotation for training course*

We are offering two-days training in secretarial word-processing skills for students who have passed their secretarial courses. This is a specialised training course, and our fees are competitively very low for students to avail of this golden opportunity.

Quotation
Course charges: Rs. 2,000
Including VAT
Terms: Net payment, 30 days from date of invoice.

Yours faithfully,

Example—Quotations for Office Equipment

Santosh Equipments
4, Mahasena Road,
Andheri East
Mumbai
15 June 2000

Messrs Barnes & Sons
Aurangzeb Road,
Kothi
Lucknow

Dear Sir,

We thank you for your enquiry of 1 June, and have pleasure in quoting for your requirements as follows:

1) ***Godrej Secretary Desks**, as illustrated on page 3 of the catalogue, in grey and maroon shades, with 4 drawers, 1 locking, on right-hand side. Price : 3,000 each*
2) ***Steel Office Chairs**, also illustrated on pages 5 and 6, with maroon or grey padded seats, adjustable back—price : Rs. 1,000 each*

***Terms:** Less 10% trade discount and 2% cash discount for payment against monthly account*

***Delivery:** 15 days from receipt of order—carriage paid and charged.*

We look forward to doing business with you.

You can be assured of our best attention.

Yours faithfully,

A tender, usually produced in response to an advertisement, is in competition with tenders from other companies. It is an offer to supply goods or services at a certain rate, but usually needs to be set out in considerably greater details than an estimate or quotation. Often, the organisation seeking tenders will supply forms.

Tenders require careful detailing of estimated costs.

Example—Offer to Buy Assets

Dear Sir,

***Subject :** Liquidation of Assets of Parul Furnishings*

We submit the following offer to buy assets of Parul Furnishings, now in liquidation:

Unsold stock as per your	*Rs.*
List of assets	*9,50,000*
One delivery van	*2,22,000*
Office fittings items 6-9 on	
Your list of assets	*48,000*
Total Rs.	*12,20,000*

If you agree to this offer we shall pay you by cheque immediately, and make arrangements to collect these goods within four weeks.

Yours faithfully,

Example—Public Tender

Sealed tenders are invited by the Karnataka State Beverages Corporation Ltd for providing Tata Indica Taxis on Hire Basis from Travel Agencies who have registered with KSTDC, and who have minimum five vehicles in their name or in the name of the agency.

The duration of contract will be twelve months from the date of agreement.

Blank tender forms may be obtained from the office from 20 April 2002 to 28 April 2002.

An EMD of Rs. 10,000/- in the form of DD/Pay Order drawn in favour of the Corporation should be furnished along with the tender.

The last date for receipt of duly filled in tenders is 19 May 2002 up to 3.00 p.m.

The tenders will be opened on 20 May 2002 at 3.30 p.m. in the presence of available tenderers.

Further details can be had from the office:

Sd/-
Senior General Manager
(Hr & Adm.)

INVOICES

An invoice is a demand for payment, sent out either before or after delivery of goods or services.

Example—Invoice for Re-laying Garden Path

Sultan Ayub
Builder
2, Koramangala Layout
Bangalore-15

INVOICE

For relaying garden path:	*Rs.*
48 pairing slabs @ Rs. 7.50 each	*360.00*
Turf	*120.00*
Labour, as agreed	*150.00*
	630.00
VAT	*50.00*
Total Rs	*680.00*

Example—Error in Invoice

3 March 2000

Dear Sirs,

***Subject:** Error in Invoice bill*

We have received a copy of your bill no. 25 ST dated 20 February 2000 for Rs. 15,000/-.

We find that you have given us a discount of only 20% instead of 25% as promised by you.

We are returning the bill for necessary correction, and shall send our payment as soon as we receive the correct bill.

Thanking you

Yours faithfully,

PRICE INCREASES

A price increase of any product is never a welcome situation. When giving the bad news, make sure that you:

1. write well in advance.
2. give the date from which the price rise becomes effective.
3. specify exactly what is going up in price, and by how much.
4. explain the reason for the price increase, and pass on your regrets for the inconvenience.

To: All sales representatives and agents

From ; Sunil Mehta, Sales Manager

<u>PRICE INCREASES</u>

Please note the price increases with effect from Monday, April 4, 2005.

All types of notebooks: 10% on list price.

All types of pens: 12% on list price

All types of paper: 15% on list price

Full details of the new prices are given on the attached sheet of paper.

The increases are a result of increased production cost of stationery items as well as the hike in petrol charges that have affected transport costs.

Kindly warn customers that if current conditions continue we shall have to consider increasing prices again within the nest six months.

PLACING AND CANCELLING ORDERS

Orders are placed after enquiries are made, and then offers and quotations are accepted by the customer. Letters expressing the acceptance of the offer are also treated as orders. Orders are also placed in response to advertisements and circulars.

Make sure to include all the details about the quality of goods, their sizes, etc. Mention must be made of possible price changes. Reference must be made explicitly clear about the terms of payment, the mode of transport, the time and date of delivery, and other particulars.

Several big firms have their own order books which contain printed order forms. All the relevant details and terms are filled in for placing order, and sent to the manufacturers or the seller. A copy is filed and another is sent to the department concerned which checks the goods when they arrive.

Example—Printed Order Form

Order no ....Ltd.

Please supply..

....

(Quantity to be specified along with other details)

....

....

The orders goods must reach our stores within 21 days of the receipt of this letter, which may be acknowledged soon.

If the goods do not conform to the quality already advertised, these will be returned at the risk of the supplying firm.

Instructions about carriage and packing.

....

....

Payment shall be made as per terms given below:

....

....

Instructions about insurance of the parcels:

....

....

Signature

(Seal of the firm)

Example—Order for Tulip Bulbs

Primrose Horticulture Centre

Reshma Bagh

Jammu

13 November 2001

Gardenia Stores and Nursery

Nanak Sahib Chowk,

Amritsar

Dear Sirs,

We thank you for your quotation of 18 October 2000.

We would be glad if you could supply us 50 tulip bulbs that bear red flowers, 20 bulbs that bear yellow flowers, and 15 bulbs that bear blue flowers.

It is important that they reach us at the earliest, as we need to plant them immediately.

We reserve the right to reject them should they be delivered after 20 days.

We hope you can do the needful immediately as we plan to place orders for seeds and other bulbs at a future date.

Yours faithfully,

Example—Inability to Execute Order in Full

Music Corner

Commercial Street,

Ooty - 1

Mrs. Seema Shanker
"Mountview",
Fairbanks
Coonoor -1

Dear Madam,

We thank you for your order of 20 cassettes and 10 compact discs.

We regret that we are unable to execute your order in full as some of the cassettes and CDs that you have asked for are out of stock.

We will send you whatever is available with us right now. We will inform you when we receive the other cassettes and CDs from the wholesalers.

If this is satisfactory, please confirm your order.

Yours faithfully,

Example—A Trial Order

Neema Soap Manufacturers
Adina Campus Area,
Belgaum
9 October 2000

Dhr uva General Merchants
15 , Gandhi Nagar Circle,
Hubli -50

Dear Sirs,

Thank you for your circular highlighting the launch of your new soap powder Neema, and soap cakes Neeman.

Please supply the following on a trial basis:

1) 50 cakes of Neeman

2) 50 packets of Neema soap powder.

We shall be grateful if you allow us at least 15% commission, as we have to give at least 10% commission to our agents who will be out to popularise your products.

The amount of invoice may please be covered by drawing upon us at 14 days after sight.

Also please confirm if you accept our order on the terms mentioned above.

We would like to reiterate once again that this may please be treated as a trial order. We may place bulk orders if the customers are satisfied with your products.

Yours faithfully,

Example—Cancellation of an Order

Krishnaswami Traders
Sayyiji Road
Mysore - 2
5 January 2000

Titagur Paper Mills
Civil Lines
Allahabad

Dear Sir,

Subject: *For the attention of Mr. C. Narain.*

We regret to say that our order for the supply of 500 sheets of Waterman Paper sent on 5 November 1996 has so far not been executed.

Since we wanted the goods within a fortnight, as mentioned in my letter, and as these have been delayed by two months, we are compelled to get our order cancelled.

If we now receive the goods, we will not accept them.

Yours faithfully,

CREDIT LETTERS

Credit letters deal with trade references and status enquiries. Most business is done on a credit business.

Credit correspondence includes requests for credit information, responses to credit information, requests, letters granting credit, and letters denying credit.

When to grant credit, necessary information has to be received, satisfactory arrangements have to be made with the debtor, enquiries to be made concerning the standing, character, reputation and financial status of the persons seeking credit. Commercial banks and agencies or acquaintances may have to be contacted for this. Such enquiries are generally marked as 'confidential'.

Letters asking for credit information should include the following:

1) An indication that the person or firm has been referred to them.
2) A request for information.
3) An assurance that it will be held in confidence.
4) An expression of appreciation.
5) A questionnaire, if need be, asking terms of payment, experience, etc.

Care should be taken in replies to letters of such enquiry, that the information supplied is totally objective and accurate. If you cannot give definite information, you should frankly state this. If the opinion is adverse, the firm may be referred to in the reply as "the firm you mention" or "the firm about which you have enquired" and so on.

Letters granting credit should include:

1) an expression of pleasure at opening the account
2) explanation of credit procedures

3) an offer of help or service

Letters refusing credit should include:

1) an expression of pleasure at the request
2) suggestion that sales be made on a cash basis and expressing regret at not being able to open a credit account.
3) a goodwill and selling progression

Example—Applying for Credit

Gentlemen,

We have been purchasing products from you for more than a year on a C.O.D. basis. We request that you open a charge account at this time for our mutual convenience.

If you require any information from us, please do let us know.

Please let us also know your usual credit terms.

Very truly yours,

Example - Seeking Credit Reference

Dear Mr. Mathur,

Thank you for your order dated 21 May 2000. According to your wishes, it is being processed.

This being your first order , we would like you to fill the enclosed application form to open a line of credit for you with us, and return it as early as possible.

We will send you the shipment as soon as we receive the application form.

Very sincerely yours

Examples—Seeking Trade Reference

Fabers Fabrics & Co.
2, Rajouri Street,
Lalwani Bagh,

Jallunder-1
9 June 2000

Apurva Sarees & Silks
9, Dhyan Singh Chowk,
Kotah—5

Dear Sirs,

We are happy to receive an order for the supply of Swiss Cotton fabrics to the value of Rs. 25,000.

Since this is your first transaction with us, we would appreciate if you could furnish us with the names of the banks or firms with whom you have had dealings for the past few years. This is a customary practice in our business house.

We are sure that this will help us to have good bonding and relations.

We assure you of our full cooperation with you in all future transactions.

Yours faithfully,

Example—Request for Credit Information

24 August 2000

CONFIDENTIAL

Dear Sirs,

Apurva Sarees and Silks have placed an order with us for goods worth Rs. 25,000/-. They have given your name as one of the references.

We would be grateful if you could furnish us with any information about them, particularly in regard to their promptness in payment of their bills. We would appreciate it if you let us know whether they can be trusted with a credit of Rs. 25,000.

Any information that you give us will be kept strictly confidential, and we shall be glad to reciprocate similar service whenever an occasion arises.

Yours faithfully,

Example—Giving Credit Information

Gentlemen

We received your letter dated 25 August 2000 requesting us for information about the promptness of payment by Apurva Sarees & Silks.

We can state with guarantee that we have had business relations with them for several years and have always found them prompt in their payments. We can vouchsafe for them and you can be quite safe in allowing them credit.

This is given in strict confidence, and it must be understood that we accept no responsibility in the matter.

Yours faithfully,

Example of Information about Solvency

5, Raman Road,
Banda Layout,
Jabalpur
9 September 2000

Arvind Trading Co. Ltd.
New Delhi -2.

Dear Sirs,

We are in receipt of your letter dated 31 August 2000.

Since the onset of trade depression with its evil consequences, we are exercising greater vigilance while entering into new business relations, and also enquiring into existing ones. It is therefore of great importance to us to obtain reliable information about the four firms mentioned in our enclosed list.

We will be greatly obliged to you if you could advise us on this matter. We shall send on to you substantial orders on our part.

We have conducted business with numbers 1 and 2 mentioned in the enclosed list, but we would like to know whether they still enjoy the same good old reputation for safety and solvency.

The other two are new firms unknown to us, and they desire to have on new account large quantities of goods for export to China and Japan. We desire to receive reliable information about them.

We assure you of our sincere thanks and absolute confidence.

Yours faithfully,

Example—Granting Credit

19 December 2000

Dear Mr Narasimhan,

We are very glad to send you our Useit Credit Card as requested by you. We hope it will find a pride of place amongst your other important cards.

There are many advantages you can have with this card. It provides a permanent record of your expenses for petrol and oil, you can use it for purchases of marine products, and avail of the discount available with this card when you travel by any ship or go on a cruise.

The enclosed folder gives you details about the other discounts that you can avail of. We hope you enjoy using our card.

Very Truly Yours

REMITTANCE LETTERS

These letters normally deal with acknowledging receipt of goods and making payment.

The buyer, known as the debtor, acknowledges receipt of goods received from the seller, known as the creditor, except when goods have been consigned along with a delivery note. In case the goods have not been bought on credit, the amount in the invoice should be settled soon after the receipt of the goods.

The mode of payment is decided between the buyer and the seller—down payment, credit for a time period or against acceptance.

Net cash that no discount or allowance is given; for cash means a discount of $2^1/_2$% will be given for prompt payment; 5% within a month that 5% discount will be given if payment is made within a month.

In the wholesale trade, where large sums of money are involved, payments are generally made by cheque or draft or bill of exchange.

When the debtor and the creditor have each a bank account, payment is normally transferred from one account to the other.

A collector may collect the amount of his outstanding bills either by drawing a bill of exchange on the debtor, or receiving cash on delivery (C.O.D.).

All bills and invoices should be sent immediately to enable the buyer to check the goods or services rendered, make an entry in his accounts, and arrange for an early payment.

When a trader sends an invoice, he makes it a condition that the amount as stated in it shall be paid to him by a bill of exchange.

The trader will advise the buyer of his draft at the time the invoice is sent, but he will present the draft only after sufficient time has been used by the buyer to examine and approve of the goods.

In letters advising drafts, each should be separately indicated, and the amount, the due date, and the person to whose order it is payable, should be specified.

Example—Sending a Bill

Parul Stationers
1, East Coast Road,
Cochin -2
8 June 2000

Registered rule

Life Academics

9, Porbander Road,

Ahmedabad-2

Dear Sirs,

We have today dispatched 5 sets of Remington typewriters according to your order no 912 by passenger train, carriage paid.

Enclosed please find Railway Receipt No 9717 dated 8 June 2000 for Rs. 5,000/-.

Please send your remittance as early as possible.

Thanking you,

Yours faithfully,

Example—Forwarding Remittance by Cheque

19 June 2000

Gentlemen,

In payment of your invoice of 8 June 2000 for goods amounting to Rs. 5000/- , I enclose a cheque in settlement.

I shall be glad if you acknowledge immediately after you receive the cheque.

Yours faithfully,

Example of Acknowledge of Receipt

26 June 2000

Dear Sir,

We received your letter of 19 June 2000 along with the cheque for Rs. 5,000 for which we thank you.

We shall pass this amount to your credit in settlement of your account.

We will be happy to serve you once again.

Yours very truly

Example—Acknowledgement of Slight Draft

Blackwell & Sons

20 May 2000

Rupa & Brothers

Mandya,

Dear Sirs,

We thank you for your letter of 210 May 2000 and a sight draft of Rs. 2,500 (Rupees Two Thousand Five Hundred only). This amount along with 5% discount will be passed to your credit.

We hope you will place more orders with us in future, and we assure you of our selfless service and best attention.

Yours faithfully,

Example—Regarding Advice of Bill Drawn

Rama & Sons

Itarsi

5 December 2000

Messrs. Royal Stores

Ranchi,

Dear Sirs,

We have today drawn upon you for Rs, 10,000 at 10 months in settlement of the amount of our invoice dated 25 November 2000.

Please accept the draft enclosed and return it as early as possible.

Yours faithfully,

Example—Settlement by Bill of Exchange

15 July 2000

Dear Sir,

We thank you for your letter dated 9 July 2000, as well as the five typewriters which reached here in good condition on 13 July 2000.

Your enclosed draft has been accepted by me, payable at my bank on 31 July 2000, and I shall honour it in time.

Yours faithfully,

Example—Negotiable Note

21 West Chord Road,
Madhav Nagar,
Nagpur -5
22 August 2000

Three months from this day, I promise to pay M/s Nagabhushan and Sons on order for value received, ten thousand rupees.

Example—Form of Receipt

203, Jor Bagh,
New Delhi
8 August 2000

Received from M/s Dhoni Exporters the sum of rupees ninety thousand for the twenty silk sarees.

Example—Demand Draft

Nava Traders
18, DB Gupta Marg,
Dhanbad
3 August 2000

On demand I promise to pay Mr. .... three thousand rupees for value received.

Example—Promissory Note

5, Rajaji Salai,
Chennai—1
5 April 2000

Thirty days after date, I promise to pay Mr. ....money for value received, nine thousand one hundred rupees.

COLLECTION LETTERS

It is generally the practice to make payments at the end of the month following receipt of goods. The seller sends to the buyer at the end of each month a statement of account showing balance, if any, from the previous month, goods purchased during the month, less credits given or remittances received. By this procedure both parties can quickly tally their corresponding ledger accounts.

The account is then settled if everything is straight-forward. Otherwise, if the debtor fails to pay within the specified time, then a formal reminder, that the account is overdue, is sent. Very often another reminder has to be sent along with a copy of the account. Further reminders can be sent and it may become necessary for settlement of the account being requested by a certain date. Never be impolite though, but be definite and persistent, tactful and friendly even when being forceful.

A collection letter has the following requisites:

1) A statement of the amount involved.
2) Arguments for payment.
3) An appeal or demand for payment by a specified period.
4) A sales talk, if necessary.

Regarding arguments of payment, the reasons cited could be—end of a period (fiscal year, being audited), fair play, cooperation, credit loss, cut-off supply, legal action, and so on.

Example—Collection Letter

Raheja Traders
2, Binotia Layout
Pune
14 March 2000

Messrs. Meher & Sons
Aurangabad

Dear Sirs,

Our auditors, on checking our accounts, point out that a sum of Rs. 1750/- for Bill Nos. 23 and 28 is long overdue from you.

We are closing our accounts for the financial year ending 31 March, and would therefore appreciate if you send your cheque for Rs. 1750 /- immediately.

We look forward to your continued association, and assure of our cooperation.

Yours faithfully,

Example—First Reminder

Meenu Mixies Ltd.
Madurai
10 March 2000

Messrs. Sona Electrical
Trichy -5
Dear Sirs,

This is to remind you that a sum of Rs 13,200 remains overdue in spite of the lapse of two months since you received four Meenu Mixies from us. We shall be glad if you send us the cheque to balance the amount immediately.

Yours faithfully,

Example—Third Reminder: An Enquiry

Meenu Mixies Ltd.
Madurai
20 April 2000

Messrs Sona Electrical
Trichy - 5
Dear Sirs,

We regret to say we have not received any reply to our letter dated 3 April 2000 regarding the overdue amount against your shop of Rs. 13,200.

We fail to understand the reason for your silence. It is now more than three months since you received the four Meenu Mixies from us.

It will be regrettable if this will jeopardises our business relations

We shall appreciate an immediate reply.

Yours faithfully,

Example—Threatening Legal Letter

Meenu Mixies Ltd.
Madurai
20 May 2000

Dear Sirs,

We very much regret that even after repeated reminders you have yet to send the sum of Rs 13,200 as payment for the four Meenu Mixies that you received from us.

If we fail to receive the above amount within a week of the receipt of this notice, we shall be constrained to resort to legal proceeding, and you shall be held liable to the consequences.

Yours faithfully,

LETTER OF RECOMMENDATION AND AUTHORITY

A letter of recommendation is written in the commercial world to help a business friend in establishing new business relations.

The letter of recommendation becomes a letter of credit when it requests to pay a certain sum of money to the person recommended. In this open letter the banker or merchant requests the addressee to pay for the writer's account sums of money, up to a fixed amount, to the person named in the letter.

Letters of credit are of two types: a simple letter of credit addressed to one person or firm only, and a circular letter of credit that is addressed to two or more firms so that the bearer may be able to obtain money at various places to suit his own convenience.

The addressee is notified beforehand about the collection of payment. To prevent malpractice, the bearer of the letter of credit has to sign on the letter of advice.

Each firm notes on the reverse of the letter of credit the amount (in words) paid, and the date and place of payment. The last firm mentioned in the letter of credit retains it in order to return it to the issuer, traveller's abroad are the ones who generally collect letters of credit from banks.

A letter of credit must specify:

1) The date and place of writing.
2) The address of the firm where the letter of credit is presented.
3) The name, occupation and address of the person in whose favour the letter of credit is written, along with his signature (unless it is signed on a separate letter of advice).
4) The purpose of the journey undertaken by the person accredited, and a formal introduction is necessary.
5) The total amount to be paid to the bearer, usually in return for a receipt.
6) Instructions about the mode of reimbursement by the payer.

A Letter of Authority gives someone the right or official power or permission to do something on behalf of someone else.

Example—Simple Letter of Credit

19 November 2000

Letter of Credit
No S 5252

Gentlemen,

Kindly supply to the bearer, Mr. Om Prakash Sahni, any funds that he may require to the extent of Rs. 20,000 against his drafts upon State Bank of India, Cuttack.

Each draft should bear the number S 5252.

Kindly note on the reverse of this letter the amount Mr. Sahni may draw from you.

Yours very truly,

Example—Circular Letter of Credit

15 July 2000

Circular Letter of Credit

No. VN 20020

Gentlemen,

This letter is to introduce you to the bearer, Mr. K. N. Malhotra, who is setting out on his first business trip through south India. We would appreciate it if you could advice him about the standing of various firms, if necessary.

In case Mr. Malhotra requires money, we open a credit to him with any of the firms referred to below to a total amount of Rs. 20,000 against receipt in duplicate, and we leave it to you to cover yourself for any money paid to him, plus your expenses, by a sight draft to us, or else to debit the amount to our account.

The signature of Mr. Malhotra is given below. Please endorse on the reverse of this circular letter whatever amount you pay him. This letter continues in force till 31 December 2000 from the present day.

To Messrs.

Perry & Co., Chittoor

Bajaj Brothers, Thanjavur

Balakrishna Traders, Coonoor

(Signature)

K. N. Malhotra

(Reverse of circular letter of credit , showing amount paid to the holder)

Date when paid (year)	By Whom Paid	Name of Town	Amount in Words	Amount in Figures
July 22, 2000	Perry & Co.	Chittoor	Two Thousand Rupees	Rs. 2000
Sept. 15, 2000	Bajaj Bros.	Tanjavur	Ten Thousand Rupees	Rs. 10000

Example—A Letter of Authority

Raghav & Sons
Manambadi,
Belgaum
7 September 2000

TO WHOM IT MAY CONCERN

This is to authorise Mr. R.S. Kapil Rana, bearer of this letter, to collect payments, book orders and make commitments on our behalf.

(Specimen Signature
of R.S. Kapil Rana) *(Proprietor)*

Example—Authorisation to Collect Passport

1 December 2000

Passport Officer
Chennai

Dear Sir,

Re.: Passport No. S- 5999

I authorise Mr. M. M. Bopaiah, our sales manager, to collect my passport, which was submitted to you on 20 November 2000 for renewal.

Thanking you

Yours faithfully,

(specimen signature of M. M. Bopaiah)
Attested

IMPORT AND EXPORT CORRESPONDENCE

Import and export correspondence comes into play when there is constant flow of goods from one country to another. A country exports certain goods to another country, and imports goods likewise from another country.

The import agencies include:

1) Merchants firms and joint stock companies importing goods direct.
2) Branches or agents in India of foreign manufacturers importing their own products to supply them to the traders in the company.
3) Firms of intermediaries known as 'Indent firms' or ' Indent house' importing for the local traders.

Export trade may also be either direct between the exporters and the importers trading as principals, or indirect through intermediaries or agents.

Example—Letter of Inquiry

Lucky Brothers
Dealers in Antiques
Canberra,
Australia
10 April 2000

Messrs Jat Mal & Sons
Jammu, India
Dear Sirs,

Mr. Ramchandra Guha, the Trade Commissioner of India,

informs us that you are one of the largest exporters in India. He has also sent us your catalogue.

Every month we import as much as 200 pieces of antiques from Indian merchants of Mumbai, as we are always short of requirements.

We shall be glad if you could supply us at least 250 pieces of antiquues.

We shall refer you for information respecting our business integrity and financial position to the following firm with whom we had business relations for over ten years.

Yours Faithfully,

Blackwell & Co
Canberra, Australia

Example—Asking for Catalogue and Trade Terms

Jagadish & Sons
Mumbai
9 July 2000

Messrs Stach & Bros.
Manufacturers of X-ray Films
Germany

Dear Sirs,

We are one of the biggest importers of German X-ray films in India. Our monthly imports exceed Rs. one lakh. Our regular suppliers are Brown & Sons, California, and Strasburg & Co., Frankfurt.

Our consumption lately has increased twofold, and our present suppliers are unable to fulfil our needs. Hence, we are approaching you.

Kindly let us know if you could supply us X-ray films on a regular basis.

We have been dealing with the firms referred to for more than twenty years, and they will be glad to give you any reference you require.

May we please request you to send us your catalogue along with your trade terms.

Yours faithfully,

\-\-\-\-\-\-\-\-\-\-\-\-\-\-\-\-\-\-

Example—Letter Ordering Goods

Thomas Brothers
MP Lane,
Mumbai
4 October 2000

Messrs Patel & Sons
Cloth Manufacturers
South Africa

Dear Sirs,

We thank you for your letter dated 15 September 2000.

We are also in receipt of your catalogues and samples.

We have pleasure in ordering the following:

1. Colour cotton fabrics	*50 bales*
2. Printed cotton fabrics	*100 bales*
3. Double bed-sheets (pastel shades)	*100 bales*
4. Pillow covers (pastel shades)	*50 pairs*
5. Printed curtain cloth	*30 bales*

We agree with your terms however goods should be sent in polythene covers packed in wooden cases.

Thanking you.

Yours faithfully,

\-\-\-\-\-\-\-\-\-\-\-\-\-\-\-\-\-\-

Reply to the above

Patel & Sons
Cloth Manufacturers
South Africa

10 November 2000

Messrs Thomas Brothers
MP Lane
Mumbai

Dear Sirs,

We thank you for your order dated 4 October 2000. We have pleasure informing you that the goods have been shopped on your account by S S Vayu , and the necessary invoice for Rs. 1,20,000/- is enclosed.

We have drawn on you 90 days at sight through State Bank of India, South Africa, against this shipment, and we hope you will clear the draft in time.

We assure you of our best cooperation.

Yours faithfully,

Example—Request to Send Goods on Open Account

Barnes & Noble
New York
10 May 2000

Lotus Publishers
New Delhi

Dear Sirs,

We thank you for your letter dated 25 April 2000. We agree to all your terms, but the documents should be sent direct and not against a letter of credit.

We shall remit the amount by a bank draft within 90 days after receiving the goods.

We hope you will agree to this proposal and send us the goods as per your proforma invoice.

You may also insure the goods, and charge the amount to us.

We look forward to your confirmation soon.

Thanking you,

Yours faithfully,

AGENTS AND AGENCIES

Agents , agencies and distributors play a great role in the success of a business. A manufacturer approaches retailers and wholesalers through agents, branches or travelling salesmen.

Agents approach customers with samples, extol the merits of the products, and thus enhance sales prospects. For such a task, experienced and skilful agents are required.

When someone applies for an agency, he must mention whether he has applied it in response to an advertisement, through some contact or on his own volition. He should be able to convince the manufacturers of his ability, and state his terms on which he is prepared to take up the agency. The manufacturer should state his terms for granting the agency.

Example — Application for an Agency

15 May 2000

Anurag Enterprises
Civil Lines,
Nagpur

Dear Sirs,

With reference to your advertisement in "the Indian Express" some time ago, that you require an active agent for securing orders for your books. I offer my services for the job.

I have been in the business of book trade for over ten years, and can you assure of my vast experience and dedicated service, if you favour me with your confidence and appoint me as your agent.

I have three travellers and three shops in the city, all of whom would push the sale of your publications.

All my suppliers are offering me 10% commission, and I would expect the same from you also.

I shall be glad to hear if my proposal is acceptable to you, and if so, would you kindly indicate the terms and conditions upon which you would be willing to negotiate with me? I can give you references of M/s Tilak & Co. who would provide you any information that you might desire regarding my standing, etc.

Please let me hear your views on these proposals. I look forward to your reply.

Yours faithfully,

Example—Offering Distribution of Book

National Book Traders
Mumbai
10 May 2000

Tara Publishing House
Mount Road,
Chennai

Dear Mr. Mittal,

I take this opportunity of recalling the little acquaintance we had during the Publishing Managers Course at Taj Palace.

We have now decided to add library books to our publishing programme from time to time and our first book, entitled Behind Enemy Lines by Sam Reynold, is being released on the 20th of this month.

As the book falls very much within the sale scope of your organisation, I hope you would be interested in bulk purchase of the same.

I am enclosing the circulars, giving details regarding the book. These circulars can be got printed with your address, if you so desire, at our expense.

I shall be glad to have a line in reply on the matter.

West best wishes and kind regards.

Your sincerely,

Example—Termination of an Agency

Dayal Fibreglass Works Ltd.
Jhansi,
9 March 2000

Badriprasad Works Ltd.
Coimbatore,

Dear Sirs,

With the continued strike in our fibreglass factory, production has suffered much during the last six months. Our stocks at present are extremely limited, and the sales on the average of the goods supplied to your firm annually are less than the minimum stipulations as per the agreement between us.

We regret that our Directors have decided to terminate some of the agencies in Tamil Nadu State, and your agency is one of them.

We shall appreciate if you kindly settle all your accounts with our firm. The stocks lying with you may be disposed of within six months, and no further delivery shall be made to your firm in future, because of the depleting stocks with us.

When the situation improves, we may reconsider your case, but your minimum sales should conform to the stipulations of the agreement.

Your faithfully

16

MONEY MATTERS

Banks today have become indispensable on account of the multi-dimensional services performed by them. As a financial institution, they have a great role to play in the business world. Relations with your bank are among the more nerve-racking aspects of running a business. Different kinds of insurance policies also entail some difficulties.

And then there are the problems of chasing up debts. Some large companies are known for late settlement of accounts, and so smaller clients with serious cash-flow problems.

When writing to the bank, address the bank manager or departmental head by name. If possible try to be brief, to the point and accurate. The language should be simple and not technical.

Banks provide loans, take deposits and offer facilities for withdrawal of money through cheques. They offer overdrafts to various commercial firms, advance money for commercial purposes, collect money against cheques issued, discount, bills of exchange, railway receipts and securities, issue letters of credit, provide foreign exchange, and so on.

Bank correspondence also includes letters from the head office to the branch offices and vice versa, and from one bank to another.

Example—Applying for a Loan

Madhur Trading Co.
Bhubaneswar
15 October 2000

The Manager,
Canara Bank
Bhubaneswar
Dear Sir,

We are interested in taking a loan of Rs. 30,000 against mortgaging our landed property worth Rs. 1 lakh.

The loan is required for a period of six months.

We shall be glad to have your terms as early as possible.

Yours faithfully,

Example—Opening a Current Account

28 February 2000

The Manager
Allahabad Bank
New Delhi
Dear Sir,

We wish to open a current account in the name of Messrs Jamunalal and Sons, a registered firm.

Please send us the requisite application forms. Also let us know about the formalities which have to be completed before such an account is opened in your branch.

Yours faithfully,

Example—Request for a Cheque Book

15 August 2000

Dear Sir,

We shall be grateful if you could kindly send us a cheque book having 100 bearer cheques, through our representative, Mr. Kamal Sadanand, the bearer of this letter.

Attested signatures of Mr Sadanand are given below.

Yours faithfully,

Specimen Signatures

1)-----------------------

2)-----------------------

Example—Returning a Dishonoured Cheque

Bank of Travancore
Cochin
2 April, 2000

Mr. Peter Roebuck
Boulevard Area
Cochin

Dear Sir,

We regret to say that your cheque no. PN/ 2461, dated 26 March 2000, drawn in favour of Mrs Susan Jacob for Rs. 12,500 has been returned because of insufficiency of funds in your account. The balance to your credit as on date stands at Rs. 9,225 only.

Please insure that you have sufficient balance before you issue a cheque. If need overdraft for which the usual securities have to be produced in time.

Yours faithfully,

Example—Requesting for Overdraft Facilities Account

Mahaveer Traders Ltd.
National Park Area
Bhopal
15 November 2000

The Manager
State Bank of India
Bhopal

Dear Sir,

We are expanding our business and opening two more shops in Bhopal.

We shall require overdraft facilities for Rs. 35,000 during the period of one year from today.

We propose to deposit as security our documents pertaining to the purchase of one acre of land in Coorg whose present market value is more than Rs. 2 lakhs. We do hope the security offered will be considered to be sufficient for the grant of an overdraft facility.

We look forward to an early response.

Yours faithfully,

Example—Stopping Payment of a Cheque

5, Samson Estates
Tellicherry
15 May 2000

The Manager
State Bank of India
Tellicherry

Dear Sir,

We had issued a cheque No TS/ 15521 to Mr. Ponnampet of Mr Narayan of Sunny & Co. of Tellicherry, but he has been unable to fulfil all the requisite conditions.

Therefore, we request you please not to honour the cheque makes you hear from us.

Thanking you.

Your faithfully,

Example—Sending a Cheque for Credit

Madan Chemical
Ahmednagar
9 July 2000

The Agent
Indian Bank Ltd.
Ahmednagar

Sir,

Enclosed is a cheque No 83 on Ahmednagar for Rs. 25,000 dated 8 July 2000.

We request you to kindly credit the same to our account No 33342.

Thanking you,

Yours faithfully,

Example—Issuance of Duplicate Pass Book

15, Barakhambla Road,
New Delhi
13 April 2000

Allahabad Bank
New Delhi

Dear Sirs,

I have a Savings Bank Account No. 21211 with your Bank.

I lost my passbook while travelling by bus to office.

I request you to issue me a new passbook. Please let me know if I have to complete any formalities for this.

An early response will be appreciated.

Yours faithfully,

Example—Transfer of Saving Account

13, Mahadev Nagar,
Benaras
2 September 2000

The Manager,
Bank of Baroda
Ranchi
Dear Sir,

Re: *Transfer of my Savings Bank A/c No 7272::*

I have been maintaining a savings account with your Ranchi branch for the past 15 years.

I have been transferred to Benaras. So I request you to please transfer my account to your Benaras Branch as early as possible.

My previous address was:

Om Prakash Narang
2, Civil Area,
Ranchi

My present address is given on top.

Please write to me as soon as you complete all the formalities.

Thanking you

Yours faithfully,

Example—Cancellation of an Issued Cheque

Pratima Book Shop
Agra
20 August 2000

The Agent
Indian Bank
Agra
Dear Sir,

Ref No.: *200-52*

Our cheque No. TN 52012 dated 10 August 2000 for Rs 5,000 issued in favour of M/s Sharad & Sons, has been lost in transit.

We request you to please treat that cheque as cancelled. Please do not pay any person who presents the cheque at your branch.

We have issued a fresh cheque No. TN 52024 dated 20 August 2000 for Rs. 5,000 to M/s Sharad & Sons.

This fact may please be noted.

Thanking you,

Yours faithfully,

Example—Mistake in Account

Ahmed Brothers
Faizabad
20 May 2000

The Manager,
Dena Bank
Faizabad

Dear Sir,

After receiving our passbook, we checked our current account No. 2252. We regret to say that our account has been debited with Rs. 7,115 on 10 May 2000.

We have checked all our records and also our cheque book, and have found this entry incorrect.

Please look into the matter at once, and effect necessary corrections for which the passbook is being sent.

We expect an immediate action.

Yours faithfully,

LIFE INSURANCE

A contract between two persons, whereby the insurer agrees to indemnify the insured against a loss caused by a certain event is called an insurance.

The main types of insurance are Life, Fire and Marine, and other types like Accident, Workmen's Compensation, etc.

Life insurance letters must always bear reference to the policy number, while remitting premium, the name of the person insured, the date of the premium, whether the premium is annual, half-yearly or quarterly should be mentioned by the remitter.

Example—Forwarding Policy

Life Insurance Corp. of India
Mumbai
5 April 2000

Ref. *No. : Pol./24*

REGISTERED

Mr. Sohan Lal
28 Cauvery Road,
Salem

Sir,

We have pleasure in enclosing Life Insurance Policy No. 684424 on the life of Mr. Dhyan Lal.

Please full in the enclosed stamped reply card and return it to us.

Yours faithfully,

Example—Reminder for Premium Remittance

Life Insurance of India
New Delhi
15 April 2000

Mr. Shyam Sunder
Champa Layout,
Dalhousie

Dear Sir,

Ref: *Policy No. 912562*

Your quarterly premium amounting to Rs 685 on your above referred policy falls due on the 25th of this month.

You are requested to remit the amount within a period of one month.

Yours faithfully,

Example—Request to make the Policy Paid-up

M.P. Khanna
Agartala
20 October 2000

The Manager,
Life Insurance Corporation of India
Agartala
Dear Sirs

Re: *Policy No. 61274*

I regret to state that my business being slack , I am unable to pay the premium of Rs. 3,000 on my policy.

I request you to kindly convert the policy to a paid -up one, and let me know the amount that will be due at the time of maturity.

I would like to state here that the premium falls due in January.

Thanking you,

Yours faithfully,

Example—Applying for a Loan

M. Hariprasad
Lalwani Chowk,
Kanpur
20 May 2000

REGISTERED

The Manager,

Life Insurance Corporation of India
Kanpur
Dear Sirs,

Ref: *Loan against Policy No. 937465*

I hold the policy mentioned above, and would very much appreciate if you please send me an application form for the purpose.

Please let me know if any other formalities need to be completed.

Thanking you,

Yours faithfully,

Example—Surrendering Life Policy

Banashankari-II
Bangalore
15 May 2000

The Branch Manager
Life Insurance Corporation of India
Bangalore
Dear Sir,

Re: *Policy No 10987645 -Personal Life Policy*

I thank you for informing me of the surrender value of my policy, and your valuable suggestions regarding the grant of loan against the policy.

Accordingly, I am enclosing the duly filled in loan application which may kindly be considered favourably.

Thanking you,

Yours faithfully,

Example—Notification of Policy Maturing

Life Insurance Corporation of India,
Mysore
20 June 2000

S. N. Rao

5, Sayyaji Road,
Mysore

Dear Sir,

***Re :** Policy No. 401668 -Own Life*

We are pleased to inform you that your policy referred to above matures for payment on 30 June 2000.

Please fill in the form of discharge, sign and return it to us with the policy immediately so that we may be able to arrange for payment by cheque on State Bank of India.

Yours faithfully,

Example—Submitting an Insurance Claim

R. Sunil Tandon
210, Mahavir Road,
Gandhi Layout,
Allahabad
20 November 2000

The Manager
Life Insurance of India
Allahabad

Dear Sir,

***Sub:** Policy No. 2394643*

I regret to say that my father, Badri Tandon, the holder of the above-mentioned policy, expired on 2 November 2000.

Since the policy is nominated in my name, kindly send me a cheque of Rs. 80,000 plus bonus and other facilities as early as possible.

Thanking you,

Yours faithfully,

FIRE INSURANCE

A fire insurance is a contract in which the insurer undertakes to indemnify the insured against damage to his property by fire or lightning. When a loss by fire occurs, the insured should immediately send his claim to the company for the loss, within 15 days of the occurrence, giving full particulars of the damaged property. A representative from the company then comes to assess the loss.

Example—Insurance of Goods against all Risks

Raghav & Co. Ltd.
Bareilly
2 September 2000

The Manager,
The New India Insurance Co.
Mareilly
Dear Sir,

Please insure the goods, listed and enclosed separately, in the names of Madhav & Bros, against all risks.

Kindly let us know the amount payable so that we may send you our cheque.

Thanking you,

Yours faithfully,

Example—Complaint Regarding a Policy

Vadodara
10 May 2000

The Manager,
Navodya Insurance Co.
Dear Sir,

Sub: *Policy no. 165246*

We received the policy referred to above this morning.

We notice that you have made no mention of 'loss through pilferage' this point has been specifically mentioned in the proposal form of the policy.

We are, therefore, returning the policy for inclusion of the necessary words to cover loss through pilferage also.

Thanking you,

Yours faithfully,

Example—Request for Fire Insurance

Bakshi Bazar
Gorakhpur
4 October 2000

Sunbeam Fire Insurance Corporation
Gorakhpur

Dear Sir,

Please insure me for Rs 1,00,000 at 15% per annum on the stocks in-trade at my Godown No. 5 at Deva Bhandar in Gorakhpur, against fire. The articles in stock contain wooden furniture, bales of fabrics, furnishings , etc.

Thanking you,

Yours faithfully,

MARINE INSURANCE

Marine insurance covers the risk of loss of goods due to any accident during a voyage on high seas. Nowadays transport by land and air is also covered by marine policies.

Example—Claim against Marine Insurance

Lawrence & Co.
Nagpur
11 October 2000

The Manager,
Oriental Insurance Company
Nagpur

Dear Sir,

Re: *Claim under Policy No. PN/ 4132*

We regret to say that all the 200 cases containing bales of cotton materials were damaged during the fire in the ship SS Mahadev on 28 September 2000 while the ship was docked at Porbandar port.

Your authorised surveyor has already inspected the goods that are charred beyond recognition.

Please settle our claim which works out to Rs. 1,20,000. The details are furnished below.

Cotton materials—200 cases	*Rs. 1,00,000 damaged*
Other materials damaged	*Rs. 20,000*
	Rs.1,20,000

We are enclosing the original policy and the invoice for ready reference.

We shall appreciate an early action.

Thanking you,

Yours faithfully,

Example -Insuring Goods by Rail

21 March 2000

Dear Sirs,

We wish to transport 450 cases of cashewnuts by rail from Cochin to New Delhi by 2624 Up of 10 April.

The total value of these cases is Rs. 1,25,000.

We wish to insure the consignment from the time it leaves our godown till it reaches the godown of our clients in New Delhi.

Please let us know the total premium amount payable for insuring the goods referred to above against all risks.

Yours faithfully,

Example—Request for Travelling Insurance

15 May 2000

The Manager
New Assurance Company
Patna

Dear Sir,

I am proceeding to Kenya to set up a fibreglass plant there, and would like to have travelling insurance policy for Rs. 5 lakhs.

Please send me the necessary forms for completion. Kindly let me know the total premium amount to be paid.

I shall be in Kenya for 25 days from 30th May to 24th June.

Yours faithfully,

OTHER INSURANCE POLICIES

Example—Requesting for a Floating Policy

Warrangal
15 June 2000

Messrs CDIL
New Delhi

Dear Sirs,

This is with reference to your representative's visit to our office on 12 July 2000.

We have decided to accept your quotation of 5%. Please issue us a floating policy for Rs. 10 lakhs at 5% on all goods in transit to or from our showroom to any part of India . This should be inclusive of goods in train and on railway stations, goods in transport and in godowns of transport offices, and goods in postal transit.

The policy should cover all risks from 1 August 2000 to 31 July 2001.

A cheque for Rs 500 towards premium is enclosed.

Yours faithfully,

Encl.: Cheque

Example—Enquiry about an Open Policy

Ahuja & Sons Ltd.
Jhansi
9 September 2000

The Manager,
Silversand Insurance Company
Jhansi

Dear Sirs,

We intend shipping fabrics to Malaysia regularly.

We would be pleased to know whether you are prepared to issue an open policy for Rs. 1,00,000 regarding shipments by approved vessels.

The goods will be packed and sent to Mumbai from our factory at Jhansi.

We should be glad if you please quote your rates.

Yours faithfully

17

SELLING LETTERS

Every business letter is written as if it were a sales letter.

Every answer to an enquiry might be the launching pad for future trade. Every letter of apology would be a tacit promise to do better for your clients in the future.

SELLING BY MAIL

If you engage an agency to write your advertising material, ensure that you have checked it carefully for technical matter. Your agent may be competent in the use of words and images without knowing the rudiments of your products.

Selling by mail may be expensive. So make sure therefore that your material is having its impact on the targeted parties. At first decide who should receive your sales letter. A good place to start is with existing customers. Make sure your customer lists are updated, for people do move and change jobs.

You can buy or hire customer lists from other companies. The yellow pages of phone books can come in handy too.

WRITING YOURS SALES LETTER

Your selling strategy generally governs the format of your letter. Pay particular attention to appearance and presentation, the stationery you use, the length of your text, an uncluttered and eye-catching layout.

Keep your letters short and to the point, for very people like to read everything that is sent to them, especially long letters.

Don't be patronising or overtechnical , and use superlatives sparingly even in an enclosure, sift out the really important points from the incidentals.

Give precise instructions about what to do to order your goods or services. You mighty include stamped, addressed reply envelopes.

Opening Paragraph

The most important sentence in any selling letter is the first, and often the only one that gets read. Try to keep this opening paragraph down to five lines at the very most.

Your striking statement can be something like the following:

* Save 25 per cent on your heating bills.
* We have cash to give away!
* Good news to all our regular customers! From next week we are....
* Selling Euro Vacuum Cleaners is easy. Why? because they are best you can buy. I should know. It's my job to sell them.
* If you want to present some startling facts, then you can say, for example:
* 80 per cent of homes in your area are fire-proofed. Is yours?
* Rs 10 lakh to be won!

You can also resort to pertinent questions:

* Do you want to earn Rs 10,000 a month from home.
* Do you want to shed off 5 kgs in a month without starving?
* Do you want to see Europe at a low-cost budget?

You can spice up your letter with an anecdote or an analogy.

* This is the story of a man who failed to insure his garage.
* Parry Brothers, a small company in Jamshedpur, no larger than yours, has increased its turnover by 65 per cent in the last year—and without any special offers.

The Meat of the Letter

This is where you describe, explain and convince.

In what way can your product benefit your reader? Why do you think it is better than all others?

By communicating your own enthusiasm to your reader, you will be almost there. So be clear in your mind about the strongest selling points of your product, then highlight each point in a separate paragraph.

To reinforce the credibility of your offer you can offer them a guarantee of your products, produce or offer free samples, free trials, show statistics of acceptance, and so on.

Ending Your Letter

To end on a positive note and also make an impact, find something personal that sums up the points you have already made.

Example—Selling Letter

Dear Mr. Sadhvik

I'm sure you wring your hands whenever your secretary leaves you or takes holidays.

We can help you. Most agencies give secretaries a short typing test and leave it at that. We do better by testing their typing, shorthand and other skills, and take the trouble to check their references.

So the temporary staff we provide are actually hand-chosen for the job. They are not necessarily better, but just better at the particular task you need doing.

No more spending half your day showing the new secretary how to use the word processor. No more draft accounts looking like some junior maths. exercise books. No more credit slips sent out as invoices. Just simple, smooth efficiency.

Why not let us help you the next time you need someone for a clerical post? Please call us on 292919 for full details of our staffing services.

You won't be disappointed!

Yours sincerely
Hari Baweja
Director

COVERING LETTER

Direct mail selling usually entails a leaflet, a catalogue, a covering letter, and a coupon or order form for answer.

Example—Covering Letter with a Glossy Brochure

Dear Reader,

Pest control becomes more complicated year by year. New varieties, new products, new brands.

But how useful are these things? And how safe? And where, and when, should they be used?

Safe pest-control has the answer to all these questions. Not the answers that manufacturers will give you, but the results of dedicated work by independent testers and experts.

Read the brochure that comes with this letter, and find out how best you can control pests in your garden and home safely.

Fill out the coupon, and send it off in the envelope provided, with your cheque for Rs. 125 payable to Mandana Publication.

Yours sincerely,
Ravi Prasad

PRESS RELEASES

Press releases make public to the world a new product or service. If you write your release well, most newspapers or magazines will publish it almost word for word.

Always remember that what may be news to you may not necessarily be of interest to the public at large.

Specify when you want the release to appear. Type on one side of the paper, with double spacing and a wide left-hand margin for the editors.

Use the first paragraph to give the main news, and detailed information in the following paragraphs.

Provide the name and telephone number clearly for contact for further details or confirmation. Check that all technical detail is correct and upto date.

Example—Press Release

Dharavi Books

<u>Press Release</u>	*Dharavi Books*
For immidiate release	*91, Mount Road*
	Chennai -2
23 April 2000	*Tel: 42324240*

<u>In the Limelight</u>

Dharavi Books are "Kings, Treasuries"—treasuries filled, not with gold and silver and precious stones, but with riches much more valuable than these—knowledge, noble thoughts and high ideals. Dharavi Books are India's leading publishers of Children's Books.

Recently, at the World Forum of Publishers of Children's Book held in London, a panel of judges drawn from various countries adjudged Dharavi Books as the "Best Publishers of Children's Books ".

Dharavi Books are meant for children of all ages. We publish children's literature, folk tales, classics, progressive readers, tales from far and beyond , quiz books, science books that deal with living things, body systems, great scientists and experiments, books on energy and technology, universe, inventions and discoveries, and science fiction.

We, at Dharavi, also bring out books that children can relax with—magic, ghost stories, picture crosswords.

The grammar series help children master the English language. The mathematics series will help students develop skills in the subject.

We have tried to build an incredible range of titles for different reading interests and all kinds of occasions.

Pamper your children with books from our wide range of publications. What more, if you make purchases for Rs. 250/- and above, you get two books of your choice (priced Rs. 50/-) free!

So rush now with yor orders!

-END-

For further information please contact:

Ravi Bhaskar, Manager, Dharavi Books.

FOLLOW UP LETTERS

Keeping customers is more important than finding new ones. Once you have made a sale, you must follow it up with more sales. Don't take your customer's goodwill and continuing interest for granted.

Example—Follow-up-Letter

Sachin Precision Tools
Sangli
20 June 2000

Mr. Rana Hafeez
Ahmedabad

Dear Sir,

We write to you once again on the benefits of using our latest model of precision of using our latest model of precision tools for your factory. We are sure this will be to your advantage.

You must have seen our catalogue and the price list that we sent you.

Since we have not heard from you, we presume you are still considering our offer.

We are prepared to send you more details if you require.

We would appreciate an early response.

Yours faithfully,

18

LETTERS TO STAFF

Occasionally a manager or employer might be called upon to write to a member of staff. It could be regarding a change in job conditions, pays rises and promotions, praise and reprimands, formal warning's , dismissals, and so on.

CHANGE IN JOB CONDITIONS

Any change in the terms of someone's contract must change, by law, be agreed by both employer and employee. Occasionally, you may have to reallocate staff. You must first discuss their new duties personally before confirming details by letter or memo.

Dear Sawant

I would like to confirm the details of our recent discussions, and give more precise instructions on private client reallocation within the tax department.

We decided to assign some of our clients to Rao & Sons, so that these jobs will not take up so much of your time. The ones we agreed to assign to Rao were: Shyamal Pawan, Mayura Jain, Sunita Rao, and all the Piramal family. We might as well reallocate the Savoy accounts too to Rao, as Rao & Sons had earlier dealt with them.

Your new responsibilities will be taken into account when we review the pay structure after two months.

Yours
D. Dharmesh
Head of the Tax Department

PAY RISE AND PROMOTIONS

While writing to announce a promotion or pay rise, combine details of new rates of pay and of new duties, keeping the language simple.

Dear Neeta,

Following our talk yesterday, I am pleased to confirm the details of your new job:

1) *From the first of next month you will take sole responsibility of the editorial department.*
2) *You will no longer be expected to do proofreading or writing books for children.*
3) *Your new job title will be Editor, Children's Division.*
4) *You will now report to me, Madhu Kapoor, Production Manager.*
5) *Your salary will now be Rs. 30,000 per month from Rs. 20,000 per month with effect from the first of next month.*

Many congratulations on this promotion! I'm sure you will make a thoroughly good job of it.

Yours
Madhu

PRAISE AND REPRIMANDS

A handwritten letter of deserved praise can do wonders to inspire your staff.

Dear Neeta

It is only a month since I asked you to take over as Editor of the Children's Division. But already we are seeing a tremendous progress in the quality of work from your department. Books are getting prepared in time to meet the deadline, and you certainly have shown how well you can handle the otherwise reticent artists!

Many congratulations! Keep up the fine work

Yours sincerely
Madhu Kapoor

Reprimands can be more difficult to handle as you stand the risk of alienating your staff.

The most important maxim to remember is : find something good to say if you lead with this, and then tell them where they have stepped from their normal standards. They are likely to respond reasonably to the reprimand.

Dear Susan,

We have always valued the work you do in the accounts department, and been impressed by your general efficiency. However, recently I find the ledgers do not appear to have been brought up-to-date for some weeks, and the correspondence files contain too many letters complaining of unanswered queries.

I'm sure I don't need to remind you that the pension scheme papers have to kept up to date, and that this is your responsibility. I realise that your department has had difficulties with staff changes recently, but that is all the more reason for you to give these matters extra attention.

I shall be examining these accounts again in 10 days time, and expect them up-to-date by then. Please let me know if there are any special difficulties with which you need help.

Yours sincerely
Jyotika Dhareshwar
Managing Director

FORMAL WARNINGS

You should not sack people summarily unless they have committed something gross. But prior to dismissal of any employee, he should be entitled to a formal warning, in effect, a last chance to redeem himself.

If you do decide to dismiss an employee, make sure that the formal letter of warning in reasoned and explicit. If the employee ignores the warning, you can take more drastic action.

Dear Sharmila,

I regret to inform you that your recent performance has not been up to the standards demanded of staff.

1) *Two books were handed over to you for assessment a month ago, but you have not even glanced at them. You were told that they should be reviewed within a week, as it was to be released soon, but you failed to do so.*
2) *The artists had submitted the rough layout of the catalogue for your approval, but you misplaced it. This is gross negligence. We have to get the catalogue ready for printing next week. Please look into this matter urgently.*
3) *We have received complaints that you spend a long timechatting to friends who drop in to meet you. Please warn your friends not to disturb you during working hours I expect to see an immediate and sustained improvement in your work performance. If you fail to comply, the company reserves the right to terminate your contract with the normal conditions.*

Yours sincerely
Jyotika Dhareshwar
Managing Director

Letters notifying summary dismissal are similar, but the need to observe the formalities is even greater.

19

TAKING ON STAFF

When you decide to employ new staff the advertisements in newspapers and the specification to employment agencies all need to describe the job on offer.

You have to think carefully before you decide exactly what you want to go into the advertisement—the purpose, duties and conditions of the post and so on. Then you can extract the essential parts when announcing the vacancy.

ADVERTISING FOR AN EMPLOYEE

Make sure you get your advertisements in time. The advertisement should include your company logo, your company name, a brief description of the duties, a brief description of the kind of applicant you are looking for with details of experience demanded and qualifications, a direct statement of the pay offered, a clear statement of what kind of reply is required, to whom, where, and before when. Say whether references are requested at this stage. Give any reference members.

***Secretary** required in a private book publishing company. Rs. 8,000 per month. Duties include receptionist and telephonist work. Good typing (50 wpm) and clerical skills essential. Apply in writing, with full details of previous experience, to the Managing Director , Lotus Publishers, 5 Daryaganj, New Delhi -2.*

EMPLOYMENT AGENCIES

If you are recruiting through an agency, send basic job

description with a covering letter.

Dear Mr. Bajaj,

Please note that we have the following vacancies:

1) ***Sales Representative.*** *To cover North India, and sell and promote stationery items to retail outlets and small companies. Age range : 25-30 years. Must have some experience in selling, and be well spoken and presentable in appearance.Basic salary: Rs. 8,999/- plus commission. Travel allowance Rs. 125 per day.*
2) ***Accounts Officer.*** *Commerce graduate with 4-5 years experience in computerised tallying accounting and file maintenance. Age range 25-35 years. Basic salary: Rs.10,000/ Please let us know if you have anyone suitable on your books. Please do not send any candidates who fail to meet these requirements*

Yours sincerely,

ACKNOWLEDGING APPLICATIONS

All applications should be acknowledged when they arrive. It is better to make the letter more personal by inserting the applicant's name.

Dear Miss Mehta,

Thank you for your application for the position of Editor in our Patna office. We are considering applications at present, and will write to you again within two weeks.

Yours sincerely

CALL FOR AN INTERVIEW

Dear Miss Mehta,

We have studied your application with interest, and would like to see you for an interview. We would like you to be here on Monday, 10 May.

Please call us and confirm that you will be able to attend.

We will be happy to reimburse you for your travelling expenses.

Yours sincerely,

CHECKING ON REFERENCES

It is simple to check one's references over the phone, though some companies will expect a letter first.

Dear Mr. Sehgal,

We are considering Miss Mehta for the position of Editor in out Children's Division. The post requires a general familiarity with children's books targeted for all age groups, from the fundamentals right up to senior school level.

Miss Mehta has mentioned you as a referee. I believe she worked for you as an Editor. I would be most grateful if you could give me your opinion of Miss Mehta, and any comments you have about her suitability for the post.

I can assure you that anything you say will be treated in the strictest confidence.

Yours faithfully,

OFFERING A JOB

After interviewing a candidate and finding him or her suitable for the post, you may want to offer the job to the person.

Dear Miss Sethi,

Following our discussions at the interview last Monday, I am pleased to offer you the post of Editor, Children's Division, starting Monday, 31 May 2001.

I enclose two copies of our statement of terms and conditions of employment for the post. Kindly sign one copy and return it to us as soon as possible to confirm acceptance of this post.

I look forward to welcoming you to the company, and hope that your career in our editorial department will be long, pleasant and rewarding.

Yours sincerely,

TURNING DOWN A JOB APPLICANT

How much you say depends on whom you are rejecting and how or she applied.

Dear Mr Chitnis,

Thank you for your letter of 10 May 2000, in which you enquired about a job vacancy in our company.

I regret to inform you that at present we have no vacancies, but we shall keep your letter on our files and let you know if anything suitable comes up.

In the meantime, I wish you well in your search for employment.

Yours sincerely,

20

JOB APPLICATIONS

You are a busy manager, on the lookout for a new clerk. That is all you want. What you get is a flood of applications. This involves sifting to draw up a reasonably short list.

The qualities that you want in an applicant are competence, confidence, courtesy and enthusiasm. Clarity of thought and layout, relevance and conciseness, brightness of tone without informality suggest that the applicant may be suitable for the job— just the qualities you expect in business letters that the person you finally appoint will one day have to write for your firm.

Your application is your first contact with the prospective employer. It is your opportunity to create the right impression from the outset.

The first rule for applying is to follow the instructions given in the advertisement. Supply all the information and the papers requested. Quote the source of the advertisement.

In most cases, your initial application will consist of a covering letter and a curriculum vitae, giving details of your education, training and relevant work experience.

The chances are that you are applying for more than one job, so it is worth having a standard C.V. prepared. A C.V. should be as long as you need to tell prospective employers what they want to know. If possible, keep it down to one side unless you have a great deal of relevant experience. Make sure to set it out clearly and neatly.

The first objective of any letter of application is to obtain an interview since this letter is virtually a sales letter in competition with several others. Your letter must be good enough to arouse interest.

TYPES OF APPLICATIONS

There are two types of application, a solicited application and an unsolicited application.

A solicited application is written in response to an advertisement while the unsolicited one is written for a job which has not been advertised by any prospective employer.

The advantage that the latter has is that if a candidate sends applications to several employers simultaneously, he may get a call for an interview from someone, and he may not have to face any competition.

PARTS OF AN APPLICATION

1) The covering letter.
2) C.V.
3) The samples of your work, if needed.
4) References, endorsements or a photograph where required.

The Covering Letter

The covering letter, introducing your c.v., the first thing of yours that the personnel manager will see—and one of the most important letters you will ever write.

Your ref: 29B/28/ds

Dear Sir/Madam

Technical Officer

This is in reply to your advertisement for a technical officer in today's Times of India. I would like to be considered for the post.

As you will see from the enclosed c.v., I was trained by Telecom and have completed their in-house diploma course in telecommunications. Since then I have gained fairly wide experience in sound engineering. In particular as a recording engineer and in setting up public address systems. I gained valuable experience, too, in the film industry. I would very much welcome the new opportunities that working for a large organisation such as yours would bring.

I can supply references if you need them, and can arrange for an interview at any time, but would need to have a little warning before hand.

I hope to hear from you.

Yours sincerely,

Replying to an Advertisement

Sometimes, an advertisement stresses the employer's need for someone with a good general background and with supremely experience.

Dear Sir/ Madam,

Your advertisement for a production manager in the June 5 A & M Magazine caught my attention since your requirements closely parallel my working experience. I should like to be considered for the post, which sounds interesting and challenging.

As the enclosed c.v. indicates, I have more than ten years' experience in all phases of paper production. For the past five years I have supervised a workforce of 200 people.

I should be very happy to discuss this in more detail with you. You can reach me at either of the above phone numbers, and I would be available for interview any time or day that is convenient to you.

Yours faithfully,

There are times when a more jaunty tone may be appropriate, for instance, when an advertisement asks for 'communicative abilities' or 'self-confidence', but don't overdo it.

Dear Mr. Singh,

The sales position with your company advertised in today's Indian express sounds just the kind of things I have been looking for. I hope that my C.V. will convince you that I am well cut out for such a position.

You ask for someone with initiative. I think my current employers would agree that increasing sales by 35 per cent in there years shows some initiative! And I would go further still in a larger company with a more varied range of products and wider markets.

I am quite happy in my present work, but find it a little limiting. From what I know of your company, this would not be a problem working for you. I should be happy to discuss this at an interview, but I will need a bit of notice to arrange time off from work.

May I ask you not to contact my current employer, at least for the time being. You will appreciate that it would create difficulties for me if he felt that I was dissatisfied with what I am doing at present.

Yours sincerely

Suppose you want to apply for a job, but feel that your qualifications or work experience are inadequate. Don't apologise, but instead test your other qualities; stressing your interest and zeal, and your willingness to learn.

Dear Mr. Rao,

I am applying for the post of Production Manager with your company, advertised in The Hindu on Thursday 10 May 2000.

You state that you are looking for a dynamic and fast learner. I believe that I may be a good man for the job. The job itself sounds highly motivating, especially after my three year's experience in paper production. For some time now I have wanted to move up from my present position, which has started to become routine. The job at your company sounds just the right step upwards. I am sure I could come to grips with it right away, and master the details quickly.

You will find enclosed a summary of my qualifications and working experience.

Yours sincerely

Example—Unsolicited Application for the Post of Sales Manager

Dear Sir,

I learn that your reputed firm has an opening for a Sales Manager. I also learn that you require a dynamic and energetic person who can lead a team of young sales executives. I offer myself as an ideal candidate for the post as I am confident that I can fulfil the requirements of the job. I therefore wish to submit my application for your consideration.

For the past 12 years I have been working in the sales department of which the last five years has been as Sales Manager of Reid and Taylor, Nanjangud, a private firm manufacturing suitings. My performance has been lauded as exemplary by my Managing Director, and for this I earned special pay increments twice, as the testimonial annexed show.

If given an opportunity, I assure you of my diligent and dedicated services of duties entrusted to me.

I look forward to a favourable response.

Your faithfully

REFERENCES AND BACK-UP-LETTERS

It is always sensible to cultivate people who might act as referees when the need arises—almost everyone needs a reference at some time or other. If possible, have references of people of solid social standing, such as, doctors, managers in reputable companies, principals of colleges/schools, and so on.

While completing the job description in your c.v., give the name of your supervisors or superiors at your previous and current places of work.

In the covering letter you can always request the firm not to contact your current employers, as any approach would compromise your position with them.

If you succeed in getting the job of your choice, you must write to your referees to let them know and to thank them for their help. Just remember that they are on long-term standby, as you might want to call on their services once again.

The level of formality varies according to your relationship with the referee in question.

Dear Manisha,

As you see, I am back on the job hunt. At times I wonder if I was wise in leaving your department, but the prospects sounded promising in that new post.

I'm sorry to have to bother you again, but it really is time for me to move, and I hope you will be willing to give me as good a reference as you did last time. Please let me know.

I hope that all is well with you. Please send my best wishes to anyone left from my days with the company and especially to your husband.

All the best.

The benefit of sending a letter is that it will impress the reader as evidence of your serious interest in the job. It will also show that you pay attention to the job.

Sonia Verma
19 Littleton Estate
Madikeri
9 July 2000

Clarke & Gable Ltd.
15 Cunningham Road,
Bangalore
Dear Mr. Anderson,

***Ref.:** de /291 /5*

Thank you very much for your letter of 5 July 2000. As I stated on the telephone, I shall be happy to come for the interview on 21 July 2000 at 11 a.m., and shall arrange to have my reference sent on to you direct as requested.

I look forward to meeting you.

Yours sincerely,
Sonia Varma

If you are invited to an interview and are, for some reason, unable to make the time or date mentioned, you must, of course, contact the employer as soon as possible, preferably by phone, to ask for a new appointment. Again, by sending a letter you will certainly go up a notch in the estimation of your prospective employer.

Veena Gadgil
3, Madhukar Layout
Mumbai
14 July 2000

Andrew & Co Ltd.
Santa Cruz
Mumbai

Dear Sir,

Thank you for your letter of 5 July 2000. As I said on the telephone, I am very sorry that I cannot attend the interview for the post of data entry operator on 20 July as I have to attend the funeral rites being conducted on that day for my mother-in-law but I will be able to come any time that is convenient to you on 22 July 2000.

I apologise for any inconvenience.

I do hope you understand

Yours sincerely,

When the offer for a job arrives in the form of a letter formally offering you the post, a prompt reply is called for. A phone call followed by a confirming letter is once again best.

Dear Mr. Anderson,

Your Ref.: *3005 /tn/4*

Thank you for your letter dated 10 August 2000 offering me the post of Junior Editor in your company.

I am delighted to accept the position, and look forward to starting work with you on 20 August 2000.

I accept the terms and conditions of service specified by you.

I assure you once again of my loyal and dedicated service to you.

Yours sincerely,

In case you decide not to accept the job, it is common courtesy for you to write back and state your reasons.

Dear Mrs. Sinha,

Thank you very much for your letter dated 10 March 2000 offering me the post of sales executive with your company.

After careful consideration, I have decided that I cannot accept the position.

I have been offered a seat for pursuing a doctorate course in microelectronics at Albany, New York state, and the university has offered me full aid for my research work. This has been my lifelong ambition—to do research in microelectronics—and I would like to grab this opportunity of doing so.

I do apologise for such a late withdrawal, but I received the letter from Albany just yesterday. I hope this decision of mine will not inconvenience you too much.

I would like to thank you for your confidence in my abilities.

Yours sincerely,

SOLICITED APPLICATION

Example—Advertisement for a Personnel Officer

A reputed group of companies with head office at Chennai is looking for a dynamic and progressive personnel officer with minimum 5 years, experience. B. Sc. with diploma in Personnel Management and Labour Laws.

Salary will be commensurate with qualification and experience.

Forward your resume within 10 days with passport size photograph, present salary drawn and expected salary.

Post Box no. 8324
GPO, Chennai - 600001

Example—Application for the Above

15, Sadan Bhavan,
Dayanidhi Nagar,
Chennai
10 July 2000

The Personnel Manager
Chennai-1

Dear Sir,

With reference to your advertisement in The Hindu dated 9 July 2000, I wish to apply for the post of Personnel Officer.

I have furnished details of my education, qualifications and experience in the attached sheets. I have included the names of two referees who can vouchsafe for my credentials.

I have every hope that you will consider my case favourably, and provide me with an opportunity to work with you.

Yours faithfully,

Example—Application for the Post of a Headmaster

21, 4th Main
Malleswaran
Bangalore
3 March 2000

The Principal
Leela Public School
Malleswaram
Bangalore

Dear Madam,

In response to your advertisement in Deccan Herald dated 2 March 2000 I have pleasure in applying for the post of Headmaster.

I am furnishing below the details of my qualifications and experience.

1) *I passed my MA in English from Madras University in 1985, getting 87% aggregate.*
2) *I completed my B. Ed from Annamalai University in 1987.*
3) *I completed a diploma course in School Management from Bharatiya Vidya Bhawan, Bangalore, in 1989.*
4) *I have been working as Headmaster since 1989 in Girilal Higher Secondary School. The school, is closing down shortly due to paucity of funds.*

I am confident that you will provide me the opportunity to serve your highly reputed school.

I look forward to the opportunity of having a personal meeting with you.

Yours faithfully,

Example—Application for the Post of a Typist

13, Hilton Road
London
20 June, 2000

Leads Wearing Cloth Co.
Leads,
U.K.

Gentlemen,

Your advertisement for the post of a typist in today's The Sunday

Times emphasises your need for a thoroughly competent person with sufficient practical experience.

Will you please take, a moment to consider my qualification?

I am 25 years of age at present, and have sound physique and good habits.

I graduated from Canton University in Commerce in 1996 with 80% marks in Accounting and Auditing which was my special subject.

During my college days I learnt typing at a private institute, with typing speed of 60 wpm.

Immediately after graduation Mr. Simon Craig, a well-known advocate of the High Court Canton, Employed me on part-time basis to type his legal documments.

I was also engaged to do typing work for a commercial firm on a part-time basis, and it involved a good deal of figure work.

I assure of wholehearted services, and am sure that you will find me an asset.

Thanking you,

Yours faithfully,

Example—Application for the Post of Scientific Assistant

C.V. Krishna
8, Jyothi Road,
Trisshur
15 May 2000

The Director
Bharat Pharmaceutical ltd.
Allepy,

Dear Sir,

Sub: *Application for the Post of Scientific Assistant*

In response to your advertisement in The Hindu dated 13 May 2000, I submit my application for the above-mentioned post in the light of my qualification and experience detailed below.

I passed my M. Tech Applied Chemistry from Calicut University in 1990, securing a high first class.

During my graduation and post graduation courses, I took interest in Inorganic Chemistry and fared very well.

I actively participated in all activities of scientific organisations. I was the General Secretary of the Calicut University Scientific Association, and organised several study circles for the discussion of various scientific topics. I read a paper on the 'Role of Science in Modern Society' at the annual conference of the above-named association. This paper won me appreciation of the authorities including heads of department of physics and chemistry of the university.

I have been working with BPL Laboratories for the past 5 years as Junior Scientific Officer.

I am sure that by giving me a chance to do research work in your laboratories, you will not be wasting the national wealth on an undeserving hand.

I am extremely enthusiastic to make original contribution to research in a subject dealing with Chemistry.

I hope you will give me an opportunity to fulfil the ambition of my life.

Thanking you in anticipation,

Yours faithfully,

Example- Application for the Post of a Copywriter

Dear Mr. Mohan,

Sub: *Post of Copywriter*

I am writing to apply for the post advertised in today's Asian Age.

As you will see from the enclosed career derails, I have wide experience in copywriting. During the six years I worked for Andrew Jones & Associates in the 1980s , I handled some large local accounts, including those of Bharat World Travel. Since leaving full time employment in order to start a family, I have advised Andrew Jones & Associates on a number of campaigns , and taken on freelance copywriting for the agency,

I enclose several samples of copy I have written in recent years.

I look forward to hearing from you.

Yours sincerely,

Example—Application for the Post of Field Officer

D.K. Rathod
15, Madhuban Park
Jallundar
29 August 2000

The Personnel Manager
Subhash Mills Ltd.
Surat

Dear Sir,

Sub: *Post of Field Officer*

This is with reference to your advertisement in today's Indian Express for the post of Field Officer. I wish to offer my services for the vacancy.

I completed a diploma course in textile manufacturing from Leeds University in UK in 1996.

I have since then been working for Raj Textiles Ltd. Ahmednagar, as Field Officer. I have been in charge of the progressive work in dyes in this company. I have gained considerable experience in the trade.

Given an opportunity, I can prove my mettle in your company.

Yours sincerely,

Example—Application for the Post of an Advertising Executive

2399, Mahila Colony
Mukokchang
Nagaland
15 June 2000

The Personnel Manager
Indian Express
Kolkata

Dear Sir,

Sub: *Post of Advertising Executive*

In response to your advertisement in your esteemed paper dated 14 June 2000, I have pleasure in applying for the above post.

I furnish below full particulars of my qualifications and experience.

Qualifications:

I graduated from Rochester University with a master's degree in Business Management in 1995.

I graduated from Delhi University with Advertising and Business Management as my main subjects in 1993.

Experience:

1) *I worked as an advertising executive with Baneroft Media. Atlanta for a year in 1996.*
2) *I have been working as Advertising Executive for RPG Media for four years.*
3) *I have also been freelancing as an Editor for a newsweekly brought out by Larsen & Toubro, Kolkata.*

I assure you, that given a chance, I will do my best to give you all the satisfaction you expect from an advertising executive.

Thanking you,

Yours sincerely,

Example—Application for the Post of Liaison Officer

59/2 CIF Colony
Aurangabad
9 May 2000

The Personnel Manager
Orange County Health Resort
Coorg

Dear Sir,

Sub : *Liaison Officer*

In response to your advertisement in The Times of India dated 7 May 2000, I wish to apply for the post of Liaison Officer.

I furnish below details of my qualifications and experience and other details:

Qualifications:

1) *MBA from Bangalore University*
2) *M.A. in English from Bangalore University*

Experience:

1) *I worked with Taj Tourism and Travels, Madurai, for a year as Liasson Officer.*
2) *I worked for Coramandel Spas as Personnel Manager for three years.*
3) *At present I am working for M.N. Ayurvedic Health Centre as Guest and Liaison Officer since 3 years.*

Age :

30 years

During my tenure at Coramandel Spas and at my present workplace, I have got to meet several people from various countries, and their reports about their interaction with me have been laudatory. I have sample of various reports presented at various times during my tenure there.

I have every hope that you will provide me the opportunity to prove my worth.

Thanking you,

Yours faithfully,

Example—Application for the Post of Junior Clerk

29, Guru Nanak Colony
Ambala
10 April 2000

Messrs Bhanu & Co.
Govindnagar
Ambala

Gentlemen,

Sub: Post of Junior Clerk

I wish to appply for the position of Junior Clerk, advertised in today's Hindustan Times.

I am twenty years old, and have passed 12th class CBSE Board Exam in first class from Deendayal Public School, Ambala. I have done a course in Typewriting and book-keeping.

I enclose some testimonials, and would refer you to the principal of Deendayal Public School for my character.

If you will provide me an opportunity to serve your organisation, I can assure you, I will do my best to give you satisfaction.

Yours faithfully,

UNSOLICITED APPLICATIONS

Example - A suitable Post

9C, Raja Colony
Bhopal

Deora Fabrics Manufacturing Co.
Bhopal

Dear Sirs,

I have recently completed an MBA course and am currently looking for suitable long-term employment.

My main interest at college was in dyes and fabric treatment. While at college, I held exhibitions of my work, which received favourable comments from staff and the local press.

I have only recently moved to this area. Your company was brought to my attention by one of my friends here who said that you specialise in cotton fabric dyeing, and suggested that I contact you.

While I realise that I have very much to learn in this field, I am very keen to start with a company known for its forward-looking policies.

If you think you have any suitable vacancies for me, could you please let me know? I would be grateful to speak to you at any time.

Yours sincerely,

Example—Post of General Manager

91/B Beach Road,
Cochin
1 May 2000

Messrs Nelcast Limited
Thiruvananthapuram

Dear Sir,

I learn that your reputed firm requires an experienced General Manager, and that you are looking for a person who has the wherewithal to interact with managers of various departments.

I wish to apply for the post, and hope the following requirements will be suitable for the position.

Qualifications:

1) *MBA from Stanford University, USA*
2) *MA in Business Economics from Delhi University*
3) *Diploma in Office Management*

Experience:

I worked as Assistant Manager at Messrs Jana & Co. Ltd, Chennai, for 3 years, and then as Manager for 2 years with them. My job as Manager was care of general administration and overall supervision of all the departments.

Currently working for Mayo and Company, Cochin, as Senior Manager (Personnel) since 1996.

Courses Attended:

1) *Senior Manager forum - 1 week course in Office Management held in Patna in May 1996.*
2) *A months programme on Advanced Skills in Personnel Management in 1997.*
3) *A two-day workshop on 'Labour Laws and Management' held in Udaipur in June 1998.*

I shall be glad to discuss with you any further details that you may require.

Hoping to hear from you soon.

Yours faithfully,

Example—Stenographer's Post

21, 5th Street
Indiranagar
Belgaum

The Manager
Prema Trading Company
Bangalore

Dear Sir,

Sub: *Post of a Stenographer*

I learn that you have a vacancy for the post of a Stenographer in your branch office at Belgaum.

I wish to apply for the above-mentioned post. I am a commerce graduate from Dharwar University, passing in first class.

I have done senior level courses in typewriting and stenography. I have a speed of 60 wpm in typewriting and 120 words in shorthand.

I worked for a year as Private Secretary with Lal & Sons,

Balgaum. I am currently employed as Stenographer with Satyam Sales Corporation, Belgaum.

I am sure I will prove an asset to your company, if given a chance to prove my merits.

I look forward to an early response.

Thanking you,

Yours faithfully,

Example—Post of Salesman

101, Lakeview Apts.
Kotla Area
Jaipur

M/s Dayanand Private Ltd.
Dariya Mandi,
Jaipur

Dear Sir,

***Ref:** Post of a Salesman*

I learn from a reliable source that you are in search of a salesman who is dynamic and progressive. I have the pleasure in offering my services in this capacity.

I have recently completed my graduation in arts from Maharaja College, Udaipur. My subjects were English, Economics and Political Science.

I joined Srinivasa Sales Corporation, Kotah, after my graduation, as a salesman, and worked with them for two years.

I worked for Mathias and Sons (Stationers) for a year in their Jaipur Branch office as a salesperson.

Currently I am working with Mittal Bros. Pvt. Ltd. who deal in x-ray films, film rolls and photographic goods.

I am 27 years old and hail from a respectable Rajasthani family.

I hope I get the opportunity to serve your firm in the capacity of a salesman.

Thanking you,

Yours faithfully,

OTHER EMPLOYMENT LETTERS

Example—Call Letter for Interview

Dear Mrs. Madam,

This is with reference to your application dated 5 June 2000 for the post of Sub-editor.

We shall be glad if you call on us for a personal interview on 15 June 2000 at 11 a.m.

Please bring all your original certificates and testimonials at the time of interview. Your travelling allowance for the interview will be reimbursed.

If selected you will be required to join your duties immediately.

Yours faithfully,

Example—Letter of Appointment

Dear Sir,

With reference to your interview on 15 June 2000, we have the pleasure in offering you the post of Sub-editor on the following terms and conditions:

1) *You will be entitled to draw an initial salary of Rs.7,000 plus Rs. 250 DA in the pay scale of Rs.7000-150-7150-350-7500 plus other allowances as permissible under the Company's rules.*
2) *Your appointment is for one year after which you will be absorbed on a permanent basis. During the tenure of one year your services can be terminated at one month's notice, and likewise you may also leave the job after giving a month's*

notice. After the confirmation of your service either party will have the right to do so at three months' notice.

3) *You will be entitled to contribute to our Provident Fund at the rate of 5% of your basic pay to which the company shall also contribute an equal share. The liability of the company's share of contribution will arise only when you complete three years of service.*
4) *You will be entitled to bonus declared by the company from time to time.*

If you accept the offer on the above terms and conditions, you may intimate us within a week of the receipt of this letter, and resume your duties in the Company on 25 June.

Yours faithfully,

Example—Letter accepting the Offer

20 June2000

Tata Profile
Bhopal

Dear Sir,

I thank you very much for the appointment letter dated 15 June 2000 which I received today.

I am glad to accept the offer, and shall be joining duty on 25 June 2000 as mentioned in the letter.

I accept the terms and conditions of service specified by you.

I assure you that I shall do my best to give you unstinted and loyal service.

Thanking you.

Yours faithfully,

Example – Application for Leave

14 August 2000

Dear Sir,

I have to immerse the ashes of my father in the Ganga river at Haridwar and hence I request you to grant me leave from 18 August 2000 to 28 August 2000.

Thanking you

Yours faithfully

Example—Letter of Resignation

21, Kasturba Road,
Vadodara
10 May 2000

Batliboy and Co.
VAdodara,

Dear Sir,

I have decided to resign from Batliboy and Co. with immediate effect.

As you know, I have voiced strong objections to the Board's decision to start supplying second-grade liquor to Germany, which the Board has chosen to ignore. This has made my position in the Company intolerable, and I would rather leave now than carry on in an atmosphere of ill will. I'm sure you will appreciate this is the best way.

For these reasons it would be best if I could leave at once without working out my period of notice.

Could you kindly arrange to see me later today to discuss this and other outstanding matters?

Yours faithfully,

Example—Request for Increase in Salary

15 November 2000

Dear Sir,

I have been serving your company for the past six months, working honestly and with full dedication. I have been instrumental in promoting the sales of your products with a huge profit.

My salary, since I joined your company six years ago, has been stagnant at Rs.7,000. Now I request you to kindly consider giving me a raise. Last year I had approached you for the same consideration, but my request was overlooked.

You will agree that I have proved to be an asset to your company.

Please consider my case favourably, and accordingly increase my salary.

I look forward to a positive response.

Yours faithfully,

Example—Acceptance to Increase Salary

Dear Mr. Shetty,

We have given due consideration to your application requesting an increase in your salary. The Board of Directors has decided to grant you an increase of Rs.1,500 a month in addition to the increments due. We hope this will be satisfactory.

You will be in charge of covering more areas for sales from this year onwards. We will discuss this later in the week.

We are pleased with your performance so far, and we hope you continue to be a valuable asset to our company.

Yours faithfully,

Example—Chargesheet to an Employer

9 July 2000

Dear Mr. Harish,

We have received complaint from an aggrieved party that they are unhappy with your services, and have given the following reasons:

1) *You failed to include any of the records from our Light Classical selection, as requested in the party's phone call of June 2000, and acknowledged by them the next day.*
2) *The pressing of 'Songs from the Musical's, of which our delivery contained ten copies, appears to have gone wrong. The party has returned the discs to us, complaining of too many scratches on them. How did the scratches appears? Either you were careless while packing them, or were negligent in handling them before delivery. You must appreciate that for us customer satisfaction is crucial in the record retail business. This is not the first time we have had complaints of your careless and disinterested behaviour.*

You are directed to show cause why your services should not be terminated immediately.Your reply must reach us within 24 hours of your receiving this show cause notice, failing which it will be presumed that you have confessed your guilt, and that you cannot explain your position.

Yours faithfully,

Example—Testimonials from Employer

TO WHOM IT MAY CONCERN

This is to certify that Mr. Shahid Ibrahim was employed as Assistant Manager in this concern from 1999 to 2004.

During the course of his employment with us, we found him honest, sincere and hardworking. Mr. Shahid Ibrahim would be a very valuable asset indeed for any concern, and we would be pleased to recommended him for a responsible post.

We had to dispense with his services as we closed our business in Srinagar in view of the setting up of our new plant in Dubai for which we already have an Assistant Manager.

R. Mathur

Managing Director

21

LETTERS TO THE MEDIA

When you feel strongly about a particular issue, it is always worth writing to the media with your opinions. Such a letter will get the attention of the editor though he may not publish it. If there are several letters of the same view, they can influence the coverage or prominence that newspapers or radio or television stations give to events.

You should know to whom you should write. If you want to write, say, about different stereo systems, go for a magazine that specialises in that subject.

For matters of local importance write to local newspapers, and for those that need to draw public attention nationwide consider writing to the newspapers or magazines that have wider circulation.

Remember that tabloids are unlikely to be interested in your observations on international corporate finance, while the more serious newspapers will hardly give consideration to your memories of schooldays with a celebrity.

WHOM TO WRITE TO

Generally, letters written to newspapers or magazines should be sent to the Editor, and open *Sir* or *Dear Sir* (or *Madam*). With broadcasting companies the options are wider. You can write to *The Producer* of a particular programme, especially if you wish to make comments on the programme itself or, in the case of some current affairs programmes, if you want to raise points on wider issues.

Remember too that certain programmes are solely devoted to listeners views.

SOME DO'S AND DON'TS

The editorial offices of newspapers receive a lot of mail. So you will have to make your letter stand out if you want to see your letter in print.

Don't touch taboo subjects. These may depend on each paper's policy, and many may refuse to publish letters espousing religious causes or ones that they consider unpatriotic. A letter that incites violence too will be rejected. Personal attack is also taboo. About politicians and public figures, you can air your views about their public lives but not about their private affairs.

Instead of making blanket comments on great political events, confine yourself rather to particular aspects of an issue.

Don't accuse the paper of political bias. You may certainly state that a particular article presented a partial view, but don't extend your criticism to the paper as a whole.

Do always pay attention to layout and neatness. Give your address and make sure your name can be read.

Write to monthlies and weeklies well before the issues go to press. Write to dailies as soon as possible.

Do choose a paper that is generally sympathetic to the views you are expressing. Suppose one of your local papers is publishing a lot of articles about local amenities. That is the one to write to if you are lobbying for a new sports centre.

At the outset say why you are writing. The simplest method is to state what you think in the first sentence, and why you think it, in the second.

Do back your opinions with hard evidence. And state your credentials, state your interests too, as this makes it more likely that your letter will be printed—if only to provoke a response.

Do be brief. Specify your complaint or argument clearly and crisply. Name only your most important points and arguments. If there are ten good reasons for a plan, choose the best five.

Do make your letter interesting, lively and readable. Present yourself as calm, rational, decent and tolerant. Do remember that editors often extract from, rearrange or reword letters, careful not to distort what you say.

Example—Plea to Save the Countryside

Dear Sir,

Over the last 20 years we have seen our small countryside being sucked into suburban sprawl and former local beauty spots disappearing under concrete.

Now we have only the small meadows of what used to be Golden Farm left as havens for picnickers, play and walking. If the proposal before the council (reported in your paper dated 5 July 2000) to turn the firm into an industrial estate goes ahead, even that will be lost.

Why are the council so taken with this plan. This town has room enough for building on the old courtyard at the station, for instance, or along the Kotagiri Road. But Golden Farm is unique.

So I beg the council: Save our countryside for local residents, for their children, and for generations still to come.

Yours faithfully,

Example—frequent Power Failures

Dear Sir,

Lately there have been frequent power failure in Green Park area, especially during night time. The duration has been sometimes as long as six hours. Students studying for their ongoing Board exams, mothers with newborn babies, hospitals having to rely on loud generators, and so, find these unwarranted frequent power cuts quite cumbersome.

We request the Electricity Board authorities to be good enough to maintain continuous power supply in our area.

Yours faithfully,

Example—Leave the Children Alone

Sir,

It is exam time for school and college-going children. The reported incident of a second year. Commerce student jumping from the second floor of his college to end his life is very disturbing.

It is time that parents and well-wishers of the children appearing for Board exams leave the children alone. Any kind of direct or indirect reference made to link their future with the current exams will increase the stress level beyond tolerable limits.

Similar to sportspersons who play well during practice sessions but fail to perform during matches because of stress, students too suffer mental blocks in the exam-hall. It is so because, society in the guise of parents, teachers and family relations put pressure to make a mark, and anything less than that means a loss of face to all these. So, many of the children have a nervous breakdown.

So, what is of paramount importance is that the students should never lose confidence in themselves, and should not become victims of anxiety.

Given below are some hints for students to the self-answered.

1) *Tell yourself as often as you can that you are relaxed and will be able to do well.*
2) *Breathe easily, taking in as much of fresh air as you can.*
3) *Drink lots of water, if possible, from tender coconuts.*
4) *The night before the exam sleep well for at least 4-5 hours, so that the next day you will be feeling fresh.*
5) *Stop discussing your own preparations with others because*

often they derail your own confidence.

6) Trust yourself to do well.

Yours faithfully,

Example—Improvement of Libraries

Sir,

We are in the 21st century. Acquisition and exploitation of knowledge for the benefit of mankind takes precedence over anything else.

When we look upon our State-run libraries in the city as knowledge resources, we realise how inadequate and ill-equipped they are for this purpose.

Most of the books in the Central Library, for instance, are outdated and in a very unsatisfactory condition. They are not put back in the right places by the library staff, resulting in their non-availability when needed. As a result even they are as helpless as the visiting public in locating the books.

Seating arrangements are totally inadequate. I hope the authorities concerned will pay attention to the deficiencies and eliminate them.

Yours faithfully,

Example—Euthanasia : No Freedom to Die

Sir,

The two recent cases where euthanasia was not granted have drawn much media attention, the first one being that of 25 years old Venkatesh, a chess champion from Andhra Pradesh, and of Terri Schiavo from Florida, USA.

Euthanasia, a complex issue that is still being debated globally, is generally compared with the act of mercy-killing although the dividing line is very thin. Law is meant to be the midwife of justice though in practice it is not. Indeed, law and truth seem to work fundamentally at cross purposes. As per court orders, doctors had removed Terri's feeding pipe.

Today, our attitude to death is far from healthy. We condemn to death a criminal who wants to live. For those under the beastly grip of any disease, death is liberation. This pits us against moralists who cits the scriptures and say, taking life is a sin. Doctors vouch by the Hippocratic oath and politicians stand rooted to their narrow laws.

Science promises procrastination of death, but what is the use of extended life of inferior quality? What is wrong in granting medical termination of life, if it can alleviate the sufferings of people who cannot lead a normal life?

The Netherlands and Belgium are the only two countries in the world to legalise euthanasia, of course, under strict conditions. Interestingly, in Australia, suicide is not illegal and there are devices which allow the terminally sick patient himself to administer the lethal dose, thus giving no room for malpractice or misuse.

In India, mercy killing of terminally ill people is not yet permitted even if on life support stage, and the judiciary has been moved many a time pleading that euthanasia be allowed. Rejecting many pleas, the judiciary always observed that the right to life was under the Indian Constitution.

Euthanasia can be looked at as a choice about the way we die rather than as a choice between life and death ultimately. It all boils down to a fine distinction of how one looks at life—as a right or as an obligation.

Yours faithfully,

Example—The Indian Debacle

Sir,

As my face sank into my cupped palms upon the disgusting performance of our paper tigers in the Bangalore test match, I remember reading about what John Wright had said: "I came to learn of terms like swarg and narak only after I settled down in India to coach these boys but what were the paaps I had committed in my past life to be associated with such spineless lot on the earth to share shameful situations like this–again and again. I want to escape from this narak."

The likes of Waugh brothers, Ponting, Gilchrist, and the greats of yesteryear like Gary, Viv would have laughed in their sleeves thinking that it is only the Indian team which can repeat such performances with astonishing consistency.

In the midst of agony piled, it was ridiculous to read in the newspapers that the aggregate runs scored by Tendulkar in test cricket have surpassed those of Gavaskar.

It is not the victory or defeat that shatter genuine sports lovers but the manner in which they take place. For instance, if the target set was around 320 runs, and if our boys had lost in the chase, the team would have stood tall in pride. But they buckled and caved in like a pack of cards.

We need the resoluteness of Steve Waugh, the shrewdness of Ricky Ponting, the determination and calmness of Inzamam-ul-Haq to bring us laurels.

Yours faithfully,

Example—To wear Helmet or not

Sir,

I think the successive government in Karnataka acted in a slipshod manner on the vital issue of helmet rules.

Road safety is a matter of grave concern to all road-users, be it a two-wheeler or a four-wheeled automobile.

If the High Court judgment makes it compulsory for all riders to wear a helmet, and the state government puts it off or ignores it, will it not be a contempt of court?

Again, if the rule is now made applicable in one city of the same state and not made compulsory in some other city, a lot of confusion would arise, and implementing the rule will be a difficult task. If the other important states have made it compulsory to wear helmets by two-wheeled riders, it is not understood why Karnataka should hesitate in implementing the rule for some flimsy cause like election.

Let us hope, at least now the present government in Karnataka will act in a responsible manner, and implement this important legislation, putting to rest all sorts of confusion.

Yours faithfully,

Example—India Pakistan Ties

Dear Sir,

Conscious of the historic opportunity created by the improved environment in India-Pak relations, as revealed in the joint statement of Manmohan Singh and Parvez Musharraf, the two countries should carry forward the peace process, and work towards a mutually acceptable settlement of the Jammu and Kashmir issue.

It is gratifying to note that Dr. Singh and Gen. Musharraf have pledged not to allow terrorism to disturb the peace process.

Yours faithfully,

Though political comment makes up the majority of letters to the press, they welcome the leaven that letters on other subjects bring – especially if these are likely to persuade other readers to write in. You might want to offer praise or thanks, recall striking events from the good old days, intact people with shared interest and concerns, or make an appeal on behalf of a charity.

A light letter of the following kind could easily be shipped into the corner of the letters column of a national or local newspaper.

Dear Sir,

My eight-year-old is doing a school history project. The other day she came home and asked me what life was like in the Middle Ages. She didn't seem convinced by my protestations of ignorance.

But it set me thinking, and I wonder if any render could help.

1) *What is the point of teaching history to kids too young to have any understanding of time-spans involved/*
2) *When did people start calling the period between the Romans and the Renaissance the Middle Ages? I bet William and the Conquieror and the leaders of the Peasants Revolt did not see themselves as being in the middle of anything. In their times, no doubt, they were bang up to date.*
3) *We call all sorts of things 'Modern' nowdays – modern ideas, modern medicine, modern art, and so on. Won't that seem a bit laughable in a hundred years' time? Or will English have to find a new word and reserve 'Modern' to mean 'late twentieth century'?*

Yours faithfully

The media welcome feedback on their performance. But they like to get more than just complaints. You might like to offer them the occasional word of praise, or make constructive comments on their work.

Dear Sir,

Many congratulations on your new comedy series "Who did this?" At last comedy that is neither mindlessly childish nor mindlessly anarchic, and that avoids the temptation of playing for cheap laughs! At times it was difficult to tell whether the lump in my throat was from tears or laughter.

I hope the series maintains the standards of the first episode. I could do with more entaetainment of this quality.

Yours faithfully

PART III
OFFICIAL LETTERS

22

LETTERS TO OFFICIALS

Letters addressed to officials are the most formal of all. While business letters could be long winded with warm praises and compliments, official letters are written using a formal language, and always to the point, without being verbose.

Letters addressed to officials generally begin with such formal phrases as "I have the honour to call your attention", "I respectfully beg to report" and so on.

In a formal official letter, you must write the name, titles and designation of the official to whom you are writing.
For example.

> *To*
>
> *Shri M.N. Nadig, M.A., I.A.S.,*
>
> *Collector.*
>
> *Ooty*

The letter then begins with the very formal *Sir* (*Not Dear Sir or My dear Sir*).

Letters to public officials and elected representatives should explain your problem briefly and clearly, but forcefully and candidly, and state exactly what you want done. Try to keep your tone light and friendly. Remember that most officials, government officers and MPs are flooded with letters, many from people who were angry or distressed when they wrote.

If the matter you wish to raise comes under the national government, or if you are not getting anywhere with the local authorities, write to the relevant ministry or official body such as the Passport Office or Vehicle Licensing Office.

Example—Application to the Deputy Commissioner

Ramsingh Verma
2, Bhairav Apts.
Meera Colony
Nagapattinam
15 July 2000

To
Shri S.N. Mandal, IAS
Deputy Commissioner
Nagapattinam District

Sir,

I respectfully beg to apply for the grant of a District Board Scholarship, to enable me to pursue my studies in a university college.

I appeared for the C.B.S.E. Board Exam of Plus II level, and passed the examination in First Division.

I belong to a respectable family. My father is the Sarpanch of our village. He has always been loyal to the Government, and several of our family members served in the Great War.

My father has limited resources and cannot afford the expenses of sending me to college. It is therefore necessary for me to ask for financial aid, if I am to have the opportunity of receiving a university education.

I enclose copies of testimonials from my Headmistress, and some of my teachers, which show that my character and conduct at school were good, and that I was a good student. I hope you will consider my case sympathetically.

Yours faithfully,

Example—Complaint about Antisocial Persons

Meena Maheshwar
15, Rangila Road,
Meerabai Nagar
Kanpur
15 May 2000

To
The Superintendent of Police
Lal Chowk Police Station
Kanpur
Sir,

I want to draw your immediate attention to the havoc done by the bad elements in our locality, Meerabai Nagar. The area is haunted by many hoodlums. They are a source of constant trouble, thinking that the long arm of law will not touch them. They tease young girls and boys. They are also known to drink and gamble, and then move about freely with knives in their hands. Last night they forcefully made the shopkeeper, who was going home after locking up his shop, to open his shop and removed some of his valuable goods.

These bad social elements commit such horrors and get away scot-free.

I request you to please pay a personal visit to this locality and see things for yourself.

Yours ever faithfully,

Example – Letter from One Department to Another in the Government

No.................
Government of India
Secretariat
Directorate of Public Grievances

Sardar Patel Bhawan
New Delhi – 110001
Tel: 23363733, FAX: 91-001-23345673
2 June 2000

DPG/I/2000/00684A)
New India Insurance Co.
Poonamallee Branch
661 Trunk Road
Chennai – 600006

Sir,

Sub: *Refund of excess amount*

Further to our letter under reference dated 30 May 2000.

You are hereby directed to refund an amount of Rs.52 (Rupees fifty-two only) to Mr. S.N. Sendil. It has been finally proved that your calculation of the insurance amount due from Mr. S.N. Sendil has not been found to be correct. In the circumstances, the insurer is entitled to a refund.

A copy of your letter addressed to Mr. Sendil may please be endorsed to this department for information.

Yours faithfully,
....
Under Secretary

Example—Submission of a Report

No...........
Government of India
Ministry of Railways
Administration Wing
Rail Bhavan
New Delhi – 1
15 May 2000

From

S.K. Jain

Secretary, Ministry of Railways

Government of India, New Delhi

To

Shri Y.K. Sanyal

Secretary, Ministry of Finance

Government of India, New Delhi

Sir,

With reference to your letter no. NT/II/5723/3A dated 10 May 2000, I am sending herewith the quarterly report of our departmental expenditure.

The reports for expenditure under plan and non-plan budget are separately tabulated.

Yours faithfully,

....

Secretary, Ministry of Railways

23

LETTERS TO MPs

Writing to your Member of Parliament is a last resort. Make sure before you write to him/her that you have already tried all other normal channels. Your MP will be most displeased if he/she discovers that before writing your letter you did not even go to the police about your next-door neighbour's rowdiness.

Also remember that there is a limit to what an MP can do. He may not have the power to make or change decisions like a ministry or government department has.

But very often they can put you on to the right or best people to deal with your business. They will write to these bodies themselves, enclosing a copy of your letter. The fact that an MP has shown interest in you will ensure that officials give your case their full attention.

Politicians receive a lot of mail. So bear in mind the following to make the politicians take notice of your letter:

1) Keep it short and neat. State clearly what you are writing about at the beginning of the letter. Lay the letter out properly. Take care over spelling.
2) Get your facts right and present them clearly. Don't make unfounded assertions about people in general.
3) If you have a special interest in the subject you are writing about, say so clearly. If you are a teacher or the president

of some organisation, then mention this when writing to your MP.

4) Give your reasons to help your MP when he/she writes back to you or elsewhere on your behalf.

5) Don't just criticise but come up with specific proposals for how the problem could be solved or dealt with differently.

6) Include essential documents or article or whatever that will put the case in context.

7) Most important of all, give your letter a personal slant. Say how the issue will affect you, the others in the community.

Example—Seeking Support from MP

15 October 2000

Sir,

I would be grateful for your help with a housing problem.

I am a widow with two teenaged children. I applied to the Housing Department of New Delhi for rehousing three years ago, but am still in my present one-bedroom flat. There has been a great amount of correspondence between me and the Housing Department, and I have filled in numerous forms and been to several consultations. They promised to do what they can, but I have not heard from them for six months.

Please would you look into the matter and give my case special attention, or at least let me knows what my chances are of being rehoused?

Yours sincerely,

Example—A Specific Bill before Parliament

15 June, 2000

Sir,

I strongly urge you to assist in having clause 24 of the Finance Bill passed in its current form.

It would be a considerable help to physically handicapped people like me to have the proposed extra Rs.1,000 tax allowance. Handicapped people have enough problems finding well-paid work. We do our best, and this proposal would give us a little benefit for our efforts.

Respectfully,

Example—General Plea for Action

29 June, 2000

Sir,

Please would you do what you can to make the police enforce the laws on selling alcohol to people under 18.

We live beside a liquor shop that regularly flouts this law, and often have to put up with youngsters making a racket outside, and worse. As parents of growing children, we do not want them to grow up with daily scenes of young drunkenness.

We have contacted the police on several occasions but they do not seem to treat the matter seriously. They usually arrive too late to find any proof or are reluctant to act.

New laws are unnecessary. We only want the enforcement of existing ones. It would need an initiative from above to persuade the police to change what appears to be their current attitude. Perhaps, a question to the Home Secretary in the House might bring this matter to wider attention.

Yours sincerely,